OLD WEST RAILROADERS

Volume 16

True Tales of the Old West

by

Charles L. Convis

Watercolor Cover by Mary Anne Convis

PIONEER PRESS, CARSON CITY, NEVADA

Library of Congress Catalog Card Number: 96-68502

ISBN 1-892156-06-7 (Volume)
ISBN 0-9651954-0-6 (Series)

Printed by
KNI, Incorporated
Anaheim, California

CONTENTS

WHY ST. LOUIS IS NOT THE U.S. RAIL CENTER   2
LAND PROMOTER (John Cozad)   4
INDIAN TRAIN WRECKING (Turkey Leg)   6
FAITH MOVES A MOUNTAIN (Theodore Judah)   8
A ROCK OF INTEGRITY IN A SWAMP OF GREED (Frederick
    Billings)   11
CLASH OF THE TITANS (Collis Huntington & Thomas Scott)   14
RAILROAD SURVEYOR (Edward Berthoud)   16
EMPIRE BUILDER (James J. Hill)   19
AN ACT OF INSANE RECKLESSNESS (Albert B. Rogers)   22
SECTION HAND IN CANADA   27
WAR IN THE GORGE   (Santa Fe & D & R. G. W.)   30
WHATEVER IS FAIR AND RIGHT (Fred Harvey)   32
MOSES OF THE MENNONITES (Carl B. Schmidt)   34
EMIGRANT TRAIN (Robert Louis Stevenson)   36
SECTION HOUSE MOTHER (Margaret Flannigan)   39
CENTRAL PACIFIC NO. ONE (Nevada)   40
BILL CRUSH'S KATY CRUSH IN CRUSH, TEXAS   44
MOUNTAIN RUNAWAY (California)   46
A LEGEND OF COURAGE (Kate Shelley)   48
TUNES ALONG LAKE FORK (Pete Ready)   51
GOLD TRAIN   54
THE GREAT HINCKLEY FIRE (Minnesota)   57
THE BROWNIES (Arthur Sitwell)   60

ORDERING INFORMATION   62

ILLUSTRATIONS

THEODORE P. JUDAH   9
ALBERT B. ROGERS   25
CENTRAL PACIFIC NO. 1   43
LAKE FORK BRANCH, Denver & Rio Grande Western   53

2

WHY ST. LOUIS IS NOT THE U.S. RAIL CENTER

But for a disgruntled employee shooting the man who fired him, St. Louis would probably be the country's rail center, rather than Chicago.

Samuel Hallett, the murder victim, was a young Philadelphian who partnered with John C. Fremont to buy a majority of the stock of the Leavenworth, Pawnee & Western Railroad. At the time Hallett and Fremont gained control in 1863, the railroad had contracted with a Canadian company to lay track.

Nothing was being done, so Hallett took over, rescinded the contract, and employed another company to lay track. The Leavenworth, Pawnee & Western was the first railroad organized in Kansas and the only one to lay track before the end of the Civil War.

When the city of Leavenworth decided that it was indispensable to the railroad's success and began making exorbitant demands for land and supplies, Hallett changed the beginning point to Wyandotte (present Kansas City, Kansas) and bypassed Leavenworth completely.

Under congressional legislation, the first company to lay track to the 100th parallel at some point between the Republican River Valley in Kansas and the Platte River Valley in Nebraska would earn the right to continue construction under the new name, Union Pacific, until it met a railroad building east from California.

Government cash bonuses, huge grants of land, and expected trade from the nation's first intercontinental railroad gave importance to the race. The government expected that three lines building west from Omaha, from Atchison, and from Kansas City would be the main contestants. The two also-rans would provide branch connections to the main line, the winner.

The northern branch was expected to connect with Chicago, although no track had yet been laid across Iowa. No one doubted that the southern branch would connect with St. Louis, as the Missouri Pacific had already laid track to Sedalia when Hallett and Fremont bought into the race.

Anticipating that their first forty miles of track would be laid by August 18, 1864, Hallett sent engraved invitations and free railroad passes to men of wealth and influence throughout the nation, inviting them to the celebration.

But the celebration never came off. While Hallett was in Washington, he heard that his chief engineer, Orlando A. Talcott, a personal friend of President Lincoln, had told Lincoln the road was improperly constructed and would not meet government requirements for the first forty-mile subsidy. Hallett wired his brother Tom to fire Talcott and kick him out in the street as soon as the engineer showed up at the office. Brother Tom, a large, burly man, did exactly that.

Talcott, a small man and handicapped by partial paralysis, bided his time until July 27, 1864. Samuel Hallett was having lunch that day with John D. Cruise at the Garno House in Wyandotte. Shortly after one o'clock Hallett got up and walked out to the street. An affable, gentlemanly man, he visited briefly in front of Holcomb's Drug Store with a group of men, which included Talcott. As Hallett continued his walk up the street, Talcott raised a heavy, repeating rifle and shot him in the back.

Cruise and others carried Hallett back to the Garno House, but he died before they reached it. Talcott mounted his horse, which he had tied nearby, and escaped.

Cruise said Talcott was never caught. Another report claimed that Talcott was arrested fifteen years later in Colorado and brought back for trial, but nothing was said about the outcome. All reports agree that Tom Hallett had beaten Talcott unmercifully, and Talcott seethed with resentment against Samuel Hallett. One report said Tom had turned Talcott over his knee, giving him "a smart spanking."

Ground was not broken for a railroad in Omaha until December 2, 1864, five months after Hallett's death. The ground-breaking celebration exhausted the treasury put together by Sidney Dillon, Thomas Durant, William Ogden, Brigham Young and other promoters for the northern branch. Another year passed before they started laying track.

Samuel Hallett was called a "man of genius, of boundless energy and enthusiasm, fertile in expedients, bold and prompt in action. Had he lived he would have been the master spirit in the construction of the Union Pacific Railway, and probably one of the leading men of the country."

But after Hallett was killed, the northern branch from Omaha overcame the southern branch's lead (apparently the central branch never got started) and reached the 100th meridian west of Kearney, Nebraska, in October, 1866. This gave that branch the right to the name, Union Pacific, and to continue on west to meet the railroad from California.

The southern branch changed its name to Kansas Pacific, built on to Denver, and connected to Cheyenne, insuring that Chicago, not St. Louis, would be the country's rail center.

Suggested reading: John D. Cruise, "Early Days on the Union Pacific," in *Kansas Historical Collections*, Vol. XI, 1909-1910.

LAND PROMOTER

The Union Pacific Railroad, hoping to connect Omaha with the west coast in the 1860s, knew the importance of settlers along its proposed line. Shipping in the goods they needed and shipping out what they produced from the land would provide the income the railroad needed to make a profit.

Getting Congress to award generous bonuses of government land for railroad construction was a necessary first step. The second step required finding the people to buy that land and build the farms, ranches, and towns that would provide business for the railroad.

John Jackson Cozad had already promoted settlement in Ohio, where he founded the town of Cozaddale. He was also a skillful gambler. After working steamboats on the Mississippi for years, he joined the gold rush and did his prospecting on California faro tables. As a necessary sideline to his chosen vocation, he learned how to use the bull-dog pistols by which gamblers enforced their right to keep their gains, however gotten.

The Union Pacific gave Cozad control of forty thousand acres of prime land where the 100th meridian crosses the Platte River. In return, Cozad would organize colonists to settle there. He started with his wife, children, family and assorted relatives and friends. The new town was called Cozad.

Cozad worked hard and settlement progressed smoothly, although a few colonists grumbled about broken promises. Now and then he left for trips to Denver, Chicago, New York, and other, unknown places. He said little about the purpose of such trips or what he did on them, but he usually returned with a new roll of much needed cash.

One of Cozad's projects was bridging the Platte River. Plum Creek, the town's main competitor to the east, already had such a bridge.

But the log and sod bridge the settlers built was washed out at first high water, along with Cozad's bankroll. Alfred Pearson, one of the dozens of workers and teamsters who built the bridge, claimed he wasn't paid. He had brought his large family from Indiana, and he desperately needed the money he claimed Cozad owed him.

In the meantime some disenchanted townspeople, still complaining about Cozad's broken promises, persuaded the Post Office Department to change the town's name. "Gould" was chosen after Jay Gould, the principal financier of the railroad at that time.

But the Union Pacific never changed the name of their station. For some years travelers must have been confused, knowing they could not buy a ticket to Gould, Nebraska. Going to that town required buying a ticket to Cozad and walking the rest of the way. One would hope the ticket agents explained how short the walk was.

The Union Pacific held firm on the town's name, and the Post Office Department finally backed down. Now it is, again, Cozad, Nebraska. The chamber of commerce claims it is the center of the largest alfalfa producing area in the world. Raising irrigated alfalfa was one of the industries started there by John Jackson Cozad.

Alfred Pearson, the still unpaid bridge worker, had his showdown with Cozad in a Cozad-owned store. When the fight ended, Pearson lay dying from Cozad's bull-dog pistol, and the land promoter fled the state, just ahead of the sheriff. He emerged in Atlantic City as Richard Lee, still speculating in land. At one time he owned or had options on all the land now occupied by the famous Boardwalk.

Eventually the Nebraska Cozads sued the Union Pacific for failing to grant them all the land they thought they had coming. The suit was dismissed, as a murder warrant kept the key witness from returning to the state.

In an interesting closure to this story, eighty-seven years after Richard Lee showed up in Atlantic City, Sandra Rice, Miss Nebraska, paraded on the Boardwalk in the Miss America contest. She walked along the same paths once followed by the founder of her home town, Cozad, Nebraska.

Suggested reading: John Carson, *The Union Pacific: Hell on Wheels!* (Santa Fe: The Press of the Territorian, 1968).

INDIAN TRAIN WRECKING

T he only known incident of Indians wrecking a train happened in Nebraska Territory on August 6, 1867. Custer's summer campaign in Kansas had proven futile; Sioux and Cheyennes continued to raid. Turkey Leg's band of Northern Cheyennes, angry at the army, wanted to get even. They decided to attack a Union Pacific train, open it up, and see what was inside. They selected a lonesome section of the track at Plum Creek, a short distance west of Fort Kearney.

Porcupine was a young warrior in the band of Spotted Wolf, leader of the attack. Porcupine explained their reasons later:

"The soldiers had taken everything that we had and made us poor. We were feeling angry and said among ourselves that we ought to do something. In these big wagons that go on this metal road, there must be things that are valuable. If we could throw these wagons off the iron they run on and break them open, we should find out what was in them and could take whatever might be useful to us."

They fastened a log across the tracks with wire cut from the telegraph line. They waited until dark when a handcar, carrying five repairmen, approached. One of the five men was William Thompson, an Englishman. The handcar derailed, and the Indians jumped up from the grass and fired their rifles. Thompson described what followed:

"We fired two or three shots in return, and then, as the Indians pressed on us, we ran away. An Indian on a pony galloped up to me. After coming to within ten feet, he fired. The bullet passed through my right arm, but seeing me still running, he rushed up and clubbed me down with his rifle. He then took out his knife, stabbed me in the neck, and making a twirl round his fingers with my hair, he commenced sawing and hacking away at my scalp. Though the pain was awful, and I felt dizzy and sick, I knew enough to keep quiet. After what seemed to be half an hour, he gave the last finishing cut to the scalp on my left temple, and as it still hung a little, he gave it a jerk. I just thought then that I could have screamed my life out. I can't describe it to you. I just felt as if the whole head was taken right off."

As the attacker rode away, Thompson saw his scalp slip from the warrior's belt. He retrieved the scalp and hid, wondering how to get to help.

Elated at their success in derailing the handcar, the Indians decided to try for bigger prey. They removed some spikes, pried a rail loose, and bent it upward a foot or two from the roadbed.

Soon they saw two lights coming up the track from the east. The Indians rode toward the lights and saw two trains approaching. They tried unsuccessfully to rope the first engine. The train derailed when it reached the bent rail, killing the engineer and fireman. The conductor ran forward from the caboose, and the Indians killed him.

The train in the rear stopped and whistled. Four or five men ran forward to the wrecked train. When they realized the entire crew was dead, they returned to their train and backed away. The Indians did not attack them.

Thompson watched the Indians derail the train, and he saw the other train leave. He despaired at ever getting away. Thompson watched the Indians tear open the cars and drag out their contents. The captured plunder included a barrel of whiskey and bolts of brightly colored muslin and calico.

After setting the train on fire, scalping the engineer and fireman and throwing the bodies into the flames, the Indians turned to sport. They tied the ends of the bolts of cloth to their horses' tails and played newly-invented games of galloping over the plains, trying to ride over and tear loose others' streamers, without losing one's own.

After the Indians tired of their games and rode away, Thompson came out of hiding. He found a pail in the wreckage, took it to the creek, and filled it with water. With his scalp immersed in the water, Thompson set out on foot for Willow Island Station, fifteen miles away. There, fellow workers dressed his wounds and put him on a train to Omaha, still carrying the pail of water with his scalp.

Henry M. Stanley, reporter who later won fame in Africa, was in Omaha. He described the scalp as "about nine inches in length and four in width, somewhat resembling a drowned rat as it floated, curled up, on the water."

Thompson went to a doctor, R. C. Moore, and asked him to sew the scalp back in place. In spite of Thompson's efforts at keeping the scalp moist, Doctor Moore was unable to sew it back on.

Thompson returned to England. Later he had the scalp tanned, and he sent it back to Doctor Moore. Moore turned it over to the Omaha Public Library Museum. The museum kept the scalp on display for many years.

Suggested reading: George B. Grinnell, *The Fighting Cheyennes,* (Norman: Univ. Of Oklahoma Press, 1963).

FAITH MOVES A MOUNTAIN

Theodore D. Judah had dreamed of building a transcontinental railroad through the Sierras for years before President Lincoln signed the Pacific Railroad Act in 1862. Born in Connecticut in 1826, Judah was a young boy when his Episcopal minister father moved to Troy, New York. Judah graduated from the Troy School of Technology and got his first job as an assistant engineer (surveyor, not train driver) on the Troy & Schenectady Railroad. A brilliant young man for whom problems were interesting exercises, not obstacles, his career soared.

At twenty-five Judah was chief of construction on the Buffalo & New York Railroad. After that road's completion, he built the "impossible" Niagara Gorge Railroad, becoming one of the nation's most celebrated engineers.

The president of the newly incorporated but still unbuilt Sacramento Valley Railroad came east in 1854 for the best engineer he could find. He hired Judah to build California's first railroad.

Building the Sacramento Valley road was routine, but Judah kept looking east at the magnificent Sierras. Now there was a challenge to match his skill! He spent off hours hiking and riding muleback into the mountains, looking for a way through the deep canyons and towering peaks. His artist wife, Anna, went along to sketch the beautiful scenery.

In 1857, with several surveys completed, Judah published his *Practical Plan for Building the Pacific Railroad*, sending copies to the president and every member of Congress. The California Legislature endorsed his plan and delegated him to present it to Congress in 1860. It never came to a vote, and a dejected Judah returned to California.

In 1861, four Sacramento merchants, Collis Huntington, Mark Hopkins, Leland Stanford, and Charles Crocker, relying on Judah's Sierra survey, formed the Central Pacific Railroad with Judah as chief engineer. They hoped to build the first railroad through the Sierras, but by October they still had received no federal aid and practically nothing had been paid in for the stock.

They sent Judah back to Congress to seek federal aid. He carried $100,000 in company stock to distribute as needed among congressmen. Judah also got himself named clerk of two House committees working on the railroad legislation, and he probably wrote most of the Pacific Railroad Act of 1862. Whether this showed skill in distribution of funds or showed a knowing congress deferring to the world's best man in building railroads in difficult places, would depend on one's point of view.

Besides federal aid in loans and land grants, the government would make the bonus payments by issuing bonds to the companies (the Act

THEODORE P. JUDAH

California State Library

created the Union Pacific to handle construction coming west) in amounts depending on the terrain crossed. For flat terrain, the amounts were $16,000 per mile; for mountains, $48,000 per mile. So, building east from the flat land at Sacramento, it became very important to the owners of the Central Pacific where the mountains started and the higher payments began.

Judah, one of the world's top engineers and a man who had spent much time in those mountains, said it was twenty-two miles from the beginning of track. There, at Milepost 22, the first granite outcroppings could be seen. Of course, it was still in the foothills — near present Roseville — but Judah was prepared to argue for that point. When Huntington and Crocker wanted an earlier milepost, Judah told them that the California Supreme Court had already adjudicated in a mining case that the mountains started at Milepost 31.

"I'm willing to argue for a point nine miles further west," Judah said. "We can point out that railroad construction is different from mining."

"It's got to be further west than that," Huntington objected. "We need that extra money."

"It's outrageous to claim a point west of 22," Judah replied. "No engineer would support that."

"Have faith," Crocker said. "We'll take care of it."

And they knew how! Crocker had formed a construction company in which the rest of the Big Four had invested. That company's contracts with Central Pacific kept the railroad's treasury depleted and Big Four pockets full. Crocker had resigned from the Central Pacific board of directors to avoid the appearance of impropriety when he formed the construction company. His place was taken by his brother, who had just been appointed to the California Supreme Court by the state governor, Leland Stanford, also a Big Four member.

Crocker was right. The Big Four took care of the problem. They got the state geologist and the state surveyor general to testify that the Sierra Nevada Mountains started at Arcade Creek, seven miles from the Sacramento River levee. The place is so flat that McClellan Air Force Base was later built there.

Faith can, indeed, move mountains!

Suggested reading: John Hoyt Williams, *A Great Shining Road* (New York: Times Books, 1988).

A ROCK OF INTEGRITY IN A SWAMP OF GREED

The building of the first transcontinental railroads with its wheeling and dealing for insider profits and widespread influence-buying in Congress made Railroad Mogul a term of contempt. The disgraceful behavior of the early titans led to the Granger movement for protection of railroad customers and to legal reforms for protection of the government and taxpayers. One man stood out in this buccaneer era of corporate organization and financing like a rock of integrity in a swamp of greed. There were certainly other honest men, and not every detail of this man's business would stand up to today's glaring searchlight, but for his time Frederick Billings was a remarkable man.

Born in Vermont, Billings graduated from its university in 1844, aged twenty-one. He read law for a time, and in May, 1848, before news of the gold discovery had reached the east, he was talking about going to California to practice law. He didn't arrive until April, 1849, but he became San Francisco's first attorney, stepping off the ship with a box of law books and his newly-painted shingle in his hand. Billings became California's first attorney general and developed its first law firm.

Handling California's two largest land title cases made Billings the state's leading expert in land law. The first, litigation over the New Almaden mercury mine — California's most valuable — made him famous. The second, litigation over the Las Mariposas grant, brought him a long friendship with the grant's owner, John C. Fremont, and acquaintance with many men he would later be involved with as a railroad magnate, himself.

Working with the Congregational and Presbyterian churches, Billings was one of the founders of California's first college. When it was moved to a new location and renamed the University of California, Billings, as president of the Board of Trustees, named its new home after a famous bishop, George Berkeley.

Politically, Billings was a Whig. Although he quarreled with other Whigs who seemed to glorify big business, he loved his party's reliance on hard work, devotion to family, and a patriotism that did not denigrate others, just as he loved the Congregational Church.

As the Civil War approached, some advocated a California republic, an independent nation on the west coast. Billings, along with Unitarian minister Thomas Starr King, with whom he shared a stump-speaking tour, and Edward D. Baker, another eloquent lawyer, is credited with saving California for the Union.

Frederick Billings was quite handsome with a high forehead, a clean-shaven face, and brown hair and eyes. In 1862 he married Julia Parmly, eleven years younger at twenty-seven. She was the daughter of a New York dentist, one of the wealthiest of his profession in the country and certainly the most famous. Frederick and Julia had seven children. Two of them, both young men, died within seventeen months of each other.

In late 1863 Billings and Julia moved to New York, a move which became permanent for the family. However in March 1865, hoping for an appointment in Lincoln's second cabinet which seemed likely to go to a Californian, Billings returned to that state. The appointment did not work out. Before he returned to New York, Billings went to Oregon to see if the area would benefit from a railroad.

By now Billings was a millionaire several times over. His old friend John C. Fremont, promoting a railroad optimistically called the Atlantic and Pacific, sent him some information, and Billings went to Missouri to look the railroad over. He made his investment and took a seat on the board of directors, which he resigned after he decided that Fremont's management did not suit him. About all he had for the venture was his name on a tiny town a few miles southwest of Springfield where he had donated a thousand dollars toward the building of a church. It would not be the last town named for the former lawyer, now railroad investor.

Billings continued to invest in other railroads, and for a time served as a director of the Southern Pacific.

In the 1850s, surveys authorized by congress had produced three possible routes for intercontinental railroads. The Union Pacific-Central Pacific built the middle route, and the southern route is basically the route of today's Santa Fe. The other route would cross the northern tier of states to Puget Sound.

The Northern Pacific Railroad, created to use the northern route, was the nineteenth century's largest corporate undertaking in North America. Congress gave it the largest land grant ever — larger than all of New England — but would provide no cash subsidies.

The opportunity to earn awards of large acreage as construction proceeded, but with no cash subsidies, put a premium on discouraging land speculation, encouraging immigration, and getting the land into the hands of persons who could pay for it and quickly make it produce crops to be hauled by the railroad for revenue. The government had agreed to terminate the rights of Indians in the existing reservations that the railroad crossed, and hostile tribes still occupied other lands that had to be crossed. These factors made for an interesting mix of problems and opportunities for the Northern Pacific's Land Department. Speed, persistence, a willingness to take risks, good management, and public promotion became more important than the graft and corruption that so marred the Union Pacific/Central Pacific construction.

In March 1870, at its first meeting in two years, Billings was elected to the Northern Pacific Board of Directors. He was soon chairman of the Land Committee, which supervised the Land Department. His service there was exemplary.

Billings was elected president of the railroad in 1879. Julia wrote that he could do more good as president of the Northern Pacific than he could as president of the United States. She also mentioned that the childrens' enthusiasm was divided between his new honor and a newly hatched canary.

The railroad had already collapsed once before, in the panic of 1873. It might have collapsed while he was president had Billings been distracted by buying competing lines, contracting too soon for expensive rolling equipment, or building unneeded stations, all of which had marked previous administrations. He kept focused on construction, not advertising land until it was available for sale.

Construction, which had been stalled, resumed again at both ends of the line with Billings as president. Daily service began to Bismarck, and both coal and cattle were being loaded at the end of track in Montana Territory.

Billings drove his people with a steady flow of letters, encouraging but demanding. "We must get a cheap line and a safe road," he emphasized.

Recognizing that tourists would one day be important and showing an environmental awareness rare at the time, Billings insisted that surveyors and construction crews inflict as little scenic damage as possible.

Billings made several trips to Washington, D. C. to avoid forfeiture of land rights, as construction was behind schedule. After he won an eight-year extension, government officials congratulated him for achieving his goal "with perfect honesty."

One of the major towns on the line, Billings, Montana, was named for this decent, honest, capable man.

Suggested reading: Robin Winks, *Frederick Billings, a Life* (New York: Oxford University Press, 1991).

CLASH OF THE TITANS

By 1877 the country's top railroad moguls were Collis Huntington and Thomas Scott. Their clash in Arizona Territory, played against the background of a double crossing United States president and bribing cavalry troops with whiskey, made Huntington number one and led to the most heavily used single-track freight route in the world.

Huntington, bound out to a Connecticut farmer when his tinker-solderer-scissors sharpening father could not support his large family, was a 27-year-old storekeeper in New York when the gold rush beckoned. He soon had a general store in Sacramento, taking Mark Hopkins in as partner in 1855. Joined by Leland Stanford and Charles Crocker and called the Big Four, they formed the Central Pacific Railroad. In 1869 the joining of that railroad with the Union Pacific at Promontory Point, Utah Territory, produced the country's first transcontinental railroad.

But Huntington, by then the power of the Big Four, was not satisfied. So he merged the Southern Pacific, which the Big Four had bought, with the Central Pacific and resolved to build a second transcontinental railroad. They had through service to Los Angeles by 1876, and then laid track to the Colorado River, across from Yuma. But they had no right of way or land grants in Arizona Territory, and they would have to trespass across Fort Yuma, a cavalry post, before the lack of such rights even became a problem.

Tom Scott, three years younger than Huntington, had a similar rags-to-power career. He had dropped out of school at ten when his father, a destitute tavern keeper, died. The boy clerked in a store and then became a helper to a station agent on the Pennsylvania Railroad. There he rose fast, becoming first vice president at thirty-seven. Like Huntington, he had an enormous capacity for work. On many nights he never went to bed, catnapping in his office chair between appointments as a stream of underlings brought him their reports.

Scott had dreams of building a transcontinental railroad as early as 1867, when the Big Four bought the Southern Pacific to thwart him. Now, ten years later, he controlled the Texas Pacific. Track had been laid from Texarkana to Fort Worth, and General Grenville Dodge, the chief builder of the Union Pacific, had been hired to continue construction west from Texas and east from San Diego.

On their first trip to San Diego, Scott and Dodge were welcomed as saviors by a populace who hated the Southern Pacific's stranglehold on California.

In 1876, when the Southern Pacific had reached the Colorado River, the battle between the two men shifted to Washington. Both men knew their way around the capital. Scott had been assistant secretary of war for the Union during the Civil War. Huntington had been buying influence since the first days of the Central Pacific. He often referred to Congress as the "hungriest group of men who ever met together." Both Scott and Huntington thought they had lined up all the committee chairmanships they needed.

Scott also thought he had an ace in the hole. New York Governor Samuel J. Tilden had apparently won the presidential election in 1876, but Republican supporters of Rutherford B. Hayes claimed foul in Louisiana, Florida, and South Carolina. Continuing the fight in the electoral college, these Republicans promised southern Democrats they would end Reconstruction and divert federal funds to the South for "internal improvements" if Hayes were elected. Southerners understood "internal improvements" to mean subsidies so the South would have its own transcontinental railroad, and the deal was struck.

So the two titans, confronting each other at the Colorado River in May, 1877, were deadlocked. Each had lavished all the money on congress that he had available. Scott, with land grants across Texas, New Mexico and Arizona Territories, and California, had the legal right to lay track, but his closest track was twelve hundred miles away in Texas. Huntington, with no legal right to even enter Arizona, was poised, with track, on the California bank of the Colorado River.

Then some Southern Pacific men slipped across the river with a generous supply of whiskey to toast the cavalry at Fort Yuma. The party lasted a week. By the time the soldiers sobered up, a new wooden bridge, complete with rails, spanned the river.

The soldiers soon realized that the local citizens were very favorable to any railroad serving their area, and the Territorial Legislature backed them up with legislation. General William Tecumseh Sherman, Army Chief of Staff back in Washington, told the cavalry to hold off taking any action against Southern Pacific.

Then Huntington shifted his effort to the president. On October 9 that fall, President Hayes, who probably wouldn't have been in office but for the deal to let the South have its own transcontinental railway, signed an executive order allowing the Southern Pacific to cross Arizona, even though it had no legal right to enter the territory..

Collis Huntington was now the biggest railroad mogul of all.

Suggested reading: David Lavender, *The Great Persuader* (Garden City: Doubleday & Co., 1970.)

RAILROAD SURVEYOR

The battle between Denver and Golden for supremacy in Colorado centered around railroad building. Edward L. Berthoud, a key figure in the struggle, supported the losing side, but he left his name on a famous pass, a tiny Colorado town, and a college hall at Colorado School of Mines.

Berthoud's French Swiss parents left Switzerland for New York in 1829, when he was two years old. He graduated Phi Beta Kappa in engineering from Union College in Schenectady when he was twenty one. He would spend most of his life as a railroad surveyor. He got an early start in railroad construction across Panama.

A fortunate survivor of the deadly yellow fever epidemic, Berthoud returned to the United States for short stints in railroad construction in Kentucky and Indiana. He moved to Leavenworth in newly-organized Kansas Territory in 1855 and surveyed township lines for the General Land Office. Then he became city engineer of Leavenworth.

He resumed railroad work, locating the Leavenworth, Pawnee, and Western, a road that hoped to divert the trade in the Kansas River Valley from Kansas City to Leavenworth. By this time Berthoud had married Helen Ferrell, a woman he had met while surveying in Indiana.

Helen's parents and brothers joined the Berthouds in Leavenworth. Ironically, they left Indiana because of a railroad panic. Gold discovery in Colorado in 1858 drew the Farrells on west, and the Berthouds followed them in 1860.

The Ferrells had settled in Golden City, a village at the foot of the mountains, just west of Denver. They operated a hotel and toll bridge, and the Berthouds joined them there.

Helen helped her mother cook in the hotel and Ed pitched a tent in the mining camps, offering his services as civil engineer.

The railroad organizers back in Leavenworth urged Berthoud to look for a route through the mountains that would connect the Leavenworth-Kansas City area directly to Salt Lake City. Tiny Golden City began to fancy itself the key to transcontintental commerce. Denver, not much larger, did not agree.

An east-west pass across the mountains in the Denver-Golden City area was hard to find. Berthoud hired noted scout Jim Bridger to help him look. The scout knew of no such pass, and was no help in finding one.

But in early May, 1861, while Bridger was searching in another canyon, Ed Berthoud almost "tumbled" into the pass that provided access to Colorado's Middle Park. The information that he brought to Golden City two days later inspired a grand banquet to celebrate the news.

With support from Ben Holladay, the stagecoach king, and William Russell of Russell, Majors & Waddell, whose Pony Express had been running for a year on the longer route through Nebraska and Wyoming, Berthoud was sent on another reconnaissance to Utah in July. Again he hired Jim Bridger, and this time Berthoud's two brothers-in-law went along.

With a pack train of thirty horses and mules, the large party of twelve found the mountains on the west side of Middle Park quite formidable. But traveling carefully and using knowledge that Bridger did have from previous travels, they worked their way to Provo on Utah Lake.

Ed Berthoud had found a way to shorten the distance from the Missouri River to California by over two hundred miles. That fall a wagon road company was organized, the corporate predecessor of the first railroad to cross the Colorado Rockies.

The Civil War hampered progress in searching out a shorter way for a railroad. Ed Berthoud served as an officer in the Second Colorado Cavalry. He saw a little combat in Arkansas, but most of the war for him was boring garrison duty along the Santa Fe Trail and into western Missouri.

Back in Golden (the town larger, the name now smaller) in summer, 1866, there was much talk of a railroad directly across the Colorado Rockies. Bill Loveland, New England born friend of Berthoud, had incorporated the Colorado Central & Pacific with five Union Pacific representatives on its board. The Union Pacific was building west from Omaha, but had not yet decided where to cross the continental divide. Should they choose lower mountains with no population in southern Wyoming or higher mountains with growing settlements in Colorado? Loveland wanted them to choose Colorado.

Ed Berthoud's first hand knowledge of the Colorado Rockies was critical. Congress had specificied a maximum gradient of 2 1/4 percent. Could a practical route be found to Ed Berthoud's Pass within that restriction? If so, Ed Berthoud would be most likely to find it.

A reconnaissance in fall, 1866, established that Berthoud Pass could be used if they built a mile of tunnels in Clear Creek Canyon and then tunneled for two and three-quarter miles beneath the pass. The Union Pacific representatives, thrilled with the results, brought their chief engineer, General Grenville Dodge, to take a look. He pronounced the route through Berthoud's Pass a good one.

But good engineering always requires the consideration of alternates. On November 7, while Berthoud's expedition contemplated Rollins Pass, where another railroad would eventually cross, winter screamed in. Just across the pass the town of Fraser would someday be built and called the icebox of America.

Wind and snow beyond imagination swept across the tundra, filled the high cirques of Middle Boulder Creek, and caused the men to turn their animals loose in the blinding whiteout, barely reaching the protection of timber themselves. The Union Pacific men has seen enough; they would cross in Wyoming.

But the Colorado Central still had another chance. Denied a part of the transcontinental route, they hoped to control Colorado commerce at Denver's expense. This was not as absurd as a comparison of the two cities now would indicate. Denver was a little larger, but Golden, at the gateway of the most productive mining region in the Southern Rockies, sat at the crossroads where plains transit became mountain transport. Why shouldn't Golden connect with the Union Pacific at a point west of Cheyenne and eliminate the proposed, more direct, easterly connection between Cheyenne and Denver? Again, Ed Berthoud would have to show the way.

Berthoud dropped everything and prepared for another survey. But in 1867 the Indians were on the prod, the creeks draining the eastern slope of the Rockies flooded, and the coffers of the Colorado Central were empty. Ed's engineering was flawless, but the Union Pacific built directly down from Cheyenne to Denver.

Ed Berthoud, an extremely competent railroad surveyor, did his part in western expansion. But today Golden, Colorado, is known for a college and a brewery, while Denver is the metropolitan center of the Rocky Mountains.

Suggested reading: Robert C. Black III, *Railroad Pathfinder* (Evergreen: Cordillera Press, 1988).

EMPIRE BUILDER

G ive me enough Swedes and whiskey," he would say "and I can build a railroad to Hell." Without receiving a cent of cash subsidies after the Union Pacific and Central Pacific had swindled the government and their own stockholders for millions, and without getting an acre of free Federal land after the Northern Pacific had been given more than all of New England, he built the best run railroad in the West. And, with constant moral support from loyal partners, he did it all alone. His name was James J. Hill.

Hill's Scotch and Irish ancestors were part of the English-speaking growth in Canada after the Napoleonic Wars. His parents followed family custom in simply naming their oldest son James. After reading a biography of Napoleon, the boy decided he'd have a middle name. He thought Napoleon sounded too presumptuous, so he took the name of the General's brother, Jerome.

James Jerome's father died on their frontier farm in Ontario in 1852, when the boy was fourteen. In 1856, with six hundred dollars in his pocket saved from four years of hard work, Hill went to New York to seek his fortune. A tour of the Eastern Seaboard failed to impress him with economic promise, so he moved on to St. Paul, a booming city on the Upper Mississippi. It was the zenith time for steam boating, and Jim Hill had his job, clerking with a packet company, even before his boat landed.

For the next eleven years Hill clerked, joined the volunteer fire department, the Pioneer Guard (a militia unit), and tried to volunteer for the Civil War even though he was not a U. S. Citizen. A childhood injury, leaving him blind in one eye, caused his rejection. During these years, Hill learned much about business by study and observation, and he realized the need to find better ways to get things done, particularly in transportation. He branched out with his own freight agency and built his own warehouse.

In 1867 Hill married Mary Theresa Mehegan, eight years younger than he. She was an Irish Catholic girl educated at a Catholic finishing school in Milwaukee. Hill's parents were Baptist and Methodist, and he and Mary lived among Quakers. Mary had ten children, one of whom died in infancy. All were raised Catholics, and Hill was on good terms with the priests who often visited the home, and was a generous contributor to Catholic causes. But he never converted to the church nor worshiped noticeably in any Protestant one.

The area between St. Paul and Winnipeg naturally developed as a single economic unit, largely because it was bound together by the Red River, second in importance only to the Nile as a northward flowing stream. For many years trade between Fort Snelling (St. Paul) and Fort Garry

(Winnipeg) was hauled in two-wheeled, ox-drawn Red River carts, with huge, solid wooden wheels on ungreased axles. Their horrendous noise frightened buffalo, even geese. By the late 1860s the carts could stop at St. Cloud, as the St. Paul & Pacific Railroad had been built to that point.

Canada became a self-governing dominion in 1867, but it was three years later, when the Reil Rebellion was put down, before trade could grow in peace.

By 1877 Hill knew more about railroad economics than any other man in the Northwest. Railroad strikes that summer closed two thirds of the country's trackage, and the civil violence which followed, coupled with a disputed presidential election resolved at the last minute over cries of fraud from Samuel Tilden's supporters, brought the country close to revolution. President Hayes had to use federal troops to restore order. Meanwhile, Hill decided to acquire the St. Paul & Pacific and extend it into Dakota, where he would build huge bonanza farms to attract European immigrants into the railroad's territory.

With three partners, two of them Canadian residents and the other a former fur trader and Hudson's Bay Company agent, Hill obtained control of the St. Paul & Pacific in 1878. He incurred a risk that could have given him debts impossible to pay in his lifetime — all this just after he had built one of St. Paul's most magnificent mansions for his growing family of five children.

Later that year the railroad was completed to the Canadian border, and the terminal cities of the old Red River trade path were now connected by rail. Hill, the partners' man on the spot, worked most nights until after midnight, concerned with such prosaic matters as getting sufficient crossties, ballast, and water for work engines.

The partners had obtained control of the railroad by buying defaulted bonds. Through foreclosure they got the stock of the company, and, in early 1879, they changed its name to St. Paul, Minneapolis, and Manitoba (usually called the Manitoba). It may have been the only North American railroad whose name matched the extent of its roadbed. One of the partners sold his stock, and the Canadian residents turned their attention to building a Canadian Pacific Railroad to the West Coast. This left Hill in charge of The Manitoba and poised to become one of America's greatest railroad men.

Hill thought trackage should be built right in the beginning — the lowest grades and the gentlest curves — and kept that way with careful maintenance. He also concentrated on reducing operating costs, passing the savings on in reduced fares and haulage rates. In some of his sections one locomotive could haul eight hundred tons. Eventually competitors were amazed that Hill could haul a ton of freight for a quarter of a cent per mile.

From 1879 to 1883 track mileage doubled, but passenger miles tripled and freight ton-miles quadrupled. Jim Hill's railroad was making money when others were going broke. He cut passenger and freight rates, while revenue and profits grew rapidly. In 1882 the railroad had thirty-five locomotives, a hundred box cars, and fifteen coaches on order, and Hill wondered if it would be enough.

Hill wanted desperately to have a transportation connection to the west coast. He became one of the founders of the new Canadian Pacific, hoping that line would give him the outlet. But national sentiment in Canada prevented such a connection with a U. S. Railroad. Hill had watched the decline of the Chicago, Milwaukee, St. Paul & Pacific and the Chicago, Burlington & Quincy, neither of which had a west coast connection, and vowed that he would get one of his own, even if he had to build it himself.

By this time, one half the normal growth (births minus deaths) of Norway were immigrating to the United States, mostly to Minnesota and the Dakotas. Even more came from Sweden, but the percentage of their population was less. Hill expected the immigrants to help build his road and, more importantly, to settle the land that would be served by the road. On top of his man-killing railroad hours, he spent many more advocating diversified farming and the necessity of raising good livestock to provide employment during the five months of the year that field work could not be done.

The Manitoba extended its track to Montana in 1887. That summer they laid track six hundred forty-three miles from Minot to Helena, the longest run of track ever built in one season by one railroad.

In 1889 Hill began the final push to make the Manitoba a transcontinental railroad. It had already reached New York through steamship lines on the Great Lakes.

On January 6, 1893, the last spike was driven, and the railroad (then called the Great Northern) took its place among other coast to coast giants. In building and operating the best transcontinental railroad in the United States, and doing it with Scandanavian immigrants, whom he respected and helped, Jim Hill earned an enduring place in the Scandanavian folklore of our country.

Suggested reading: Albro Martin, *James J. Hill & the Opening of the Northwest* (New York: The Oxford University Press, 1976).

AN ACT OF INSANE RECKLESSNESS

In 1871, four years after the Dominion of Canada was formed, Prime Minister John A. MacDonald persuaded the Colony of British Columbia to join the federation. MacDonald had to promise to build a railroad linking the Dominion with the remote colony on the Pacific.

Quite a promise! The two were separated by an empty land containing isolated settlements of Scottish farmers, Métis hunters, whiskey traders, missionaries, and fur merchants, scattered like remote islets in an overwhelming sea of nomadic Indians.

The United States, with forty million citizens, had just completed its first transcontinental railroad. Canada, with less than ten percent of that population, would have to build one a thousand miles longer. And the U. S. railroad crossed a well-mapped, well-traveled area with many towns and even a few cities. Canada didn't even know where its road would go. Some of the route had not yet been walked across. No wonder some called MacDonald's promise an act of "insane recklessness."

It would develop that most of the construction problems arose east of Winnipeg and west of Calgary. The central portion would be built much like the Union Pacific had been built in the United States.

Harry Armstrong was resident engineer on the most easterly section between Fort William on Lake Superior and Selkirk, just above Winnipeg. Once, while carrying a level on his shoulder, he waded through four feet of water lying above a twelve-inch mossy sponge. He counted nine huge mosquitos on the second joint of his forefinger as it curled around the tripod. Armstrong wrote, "Their bills sunk to the hilt on that space, and they were equally thick on any exposed part of face or hands."

This 435-mile eastern section crossed the Canadian Shield, the oldest exposed rocks in North America. When the workers were not blasting their way through hard rock, they were building interlocked log mattresses to cross muskeg sections whose bottoms swallowed up tons of earth fill. On one disastrous occasion, a sinkhole swallowed an entire train plus a thousand feet of track when the underlying muskeg warmed from the earth fill laid over it.

Even after the muskeg had been conquered and the track laid, the roadbed would creep forward with every passing train. A heavy engine pulling thirty-five cars would make the rails creep about two feet in the direction of travel.

When the builders were not laying track across the soft muskeg, they were blasting through some of the hardest rock on earth. Although dynamite had just been invented, the major explosive was nitroglycerin, its unstable parent.

Too dangerous to be carried in wagons, nitroglycerin was transported in ten-gallon cans on men's backs, most of them Irish. One fifty-mile stretch of roadway contained thirty graves of men killed by unplanned explosions. Nevertheless, the packers seemed quite cavalier about their work.

A woman homesteader watched in awe as a long column of Irish packers moved down a hill with funereal comments:

"It's a warm day, Paddy."

"That's so, but maybe ye'll be warmer before we quit tonight."

"That's so, too. D'ye want me to take a word to the Divil?"

Also:

"Where ye bound, Jack?"

"To Hell, I guess."

"Well, take the other train and save a berth for me."

In spite of the banter, the homesteader thought the men's expressions showed that they felt the bitterness of death in their very souls.

Ten years passed from MacDonald's promise before construction even started west of the Red River. By then the Canadian Pacific Railway Company had been formed, and the Dominion turned the completion of the railroad over to it, offering a twenty-five million dollar subsidy plus the grant of twenty-five million acres of public land.

The new company would have to complete the construction across the Canadian Shield, then build nine hundred miles to reach the Rockies and another four hundred and fifty miles of heavy mountain construction to reach the Pacific.

The Canadian Pacific began the construction in May, 1881, at the end of track, Portage la Prairie, Manitoba. There, the company's chief engineer, General Thomas Rosser, ceremonially turned over the first sod. He had been a Confederate cavalry hero in the Civil War, and, before that, the West Point roommate of George A. Custer.

The route originally surveyed struck northwest from Selkirk to the North Saskatchewan River. Then it left the river to pass south of present Edmonton, crossing the Rockies at Yellowhead Pass. There it turned south to present Kamloops, and then on south and west to present Vancouver.

At a short meeting in St. Paul, Minnesota, three members of the executive committee decided on a more southern route. Although ten years of surveying was being abandoned, the decision would have a momentous effect on Canada's agricultural and later-developed tourist economies. Very likely the main reason at the time was to discourage United States railroads from building feeder lines into Canada.

The new route would follow the South Saskatchewan River past present Calgary and hopefully cross the Rockies at Kicking Horse Pass. Then crossing the Selkirks would get the road to Kamloops and the original surveyed route. The resulting development of such cities as Regina, Calgary, and Vancouver made the Canadian Pacific Railway Company second only to the Hudson's Bay Company in its influence on Canada's development.

A two-man partnership in Minneapolis - St. Paul contracted early in 1882 to build the six hundred seventy-five miles in the railroad's Prairie Section. This was just fifteen miles shorter than the entire length of the Central Pacific Railroad in the United States.

Since the St. Lawrence River was still frozen, the first rails were shipped from England and Germany by way of New Orleans and St. Paul.

By the end of the season four hundred seventeen miles had been completed. But the crews had been driving steel all summer at record speeds straight toward a double wall of mountains. The decision to cross the Rockies at Kicking Horse Pass, just west of Lake Louise, was not particularly hard. But how would they get through the Selkirks into the valley of the Columbia River?

Major Albert B. Rogers would be the last man one would bet on to find the way. A prairie surveyor from the United States midwest, he had never seen a mountain. Yet the company selected him to explore the most difficult peaks in the spine of North America, where dozens of more experienced engineers had failed. But Rogers longed for fame, and James J. Hill, the most powerful man in the company knew something about human nature.

Although 52-year old Rogers had a Yale engineering degree, he was far from a typical Yale man. He seemed to live on chewing tobacco, he drove his employees like a sadist, and blasphemy spewed from his lips like a mountain waterfall. He kept a plug of tobacco in one overall pocket and a sea biscuit in another. His men swore that these items represented his idea of a year's worth of provisions.

Once, a company supervisor challenged Rogers on his idea of proper provisions for his men. "I hear your men won't stay because you starve them," the supervisor said.

"Taint so, Van."

"Well, I'm told you feed them on soup made from hot water flavored with canvas covers from old hams."

"Taint so, Van. I never did have no hams."

But Rogers' driving ambition was to have his name go down in history, and James Hill promised that if he found a pass in the Selkirks that would let the railroad through, it would be named for him.

In May, 1881, Rogers, working east from Revelstoke, had led his group into the most spectacular mountain scenery in North America. Standing on the banks of the Columbia, they looked up at a vast island of

ALBERT B. ROGERS

Glenbow Archives, Calgary, Alberta

trees, rocks, and ice, three hundred miles long. It was cut off from British Columbia's alpine world by two great rivers, the Columbia and the Kootenay.

Rogers' Indian porters, nourished on little more than fresh air and thoughts of past food, carried hundred-pound packs across immense snow bridges, where they could look down over a hundred feet to white, roiling water below. Above them, avalanche paths showed where tons of snow and ice had crushed heavy timber into match wood.

When Rogers reached a place where the waters seemed to divide east and west, his undernourished Indians could go no further, and they had to retreat. Another year would pass before they could approach the area again, and confirm that the elusive pass had been found.

Its name is Rogers Pass. It lies near the middle of Canada's Glacier National Park.

Jim Hill had also promised Rogers five thousand dollars if he found the pass. Rogers refused to cash the check that the company presented to him. He framed it and hung it in his brother's home in Minnesota, where his nieces and nephews could see it.

The Canadian Pacific Railway was completed in fall, 1885, fourteen years after its start. Albert Rogers' name has gone down in history.

Suggested reading: Pierre Berton, *The Impossible Railway* (New York: Alfred A. Knopf, 1972).

SECTION HAND IN CANADA

An anonymous writer in a London journal provides an interesting account of the life of a section hand. The writer, apparently a young Englishman, was one of an eight-man gang responsible for keeping ten miles of Canadian Pacific roadbed in repair. His section, with a clear view of blue, snow-capped Rockies, was probably in Alberta and it was the mid 1880s.

They lived in a frame house at trackside, sharing it with the gang who worked the next ten miles west. The buxom wife of the English boarding boss cooked for both gangs, and sometimes had extra work when a roving gang, working where needed, dropped in.

The pay was a dollar and a half a day for six days, with four dollars a week deducted for board. The gang on the next section west got two dollars a day. Labor was scarcer to the west, and the company elected to draw the line between gangs who occupied the same house.

The writer thought the fare excellent — beefsteak and potatoes, beans, bacon, porridge, bread and butter, sweets and pies, with tea at every meal. Sunday's fare was even better. He thought the charge — four dollars of the weekly nine dollars earned — moderate.

Rousted out at six every workday by the cry, "Come, arouse!" at seven they heard their "ganger" or boss, a burly Austrian named Joe, call out, "Now, poys, all aboord." Four men then placed their hand car on the rails, and they all got aboard with their shovels.

The car's flat platform, about two feet above the rails, provided comfortable standing room. It was propelled by four men pumping up and down on a jack lever, operated like a see-saw. Sometimes the work was nearby, sometimes ten miles distant. Then they took their dinner and laughed about going on a picnic.

Besides the boss, the gang consisted of two German brothers who had been prospecting but lost their outfit crossing the Bow River, an old Irish-Canadian with a strong antipathy toward work, a young Chicagoan — something of a dude with a toothbrush in his breast pocket — two Englishmen, and an old Irish army-pensioner overflowing with reminiscences of soldiering in India. One day the old Irishman, deciding he'd seen enough, slung his little bundle over his shoulder and disappeared to the east. Their main task was keeping the track level and firmly packed. Sometimes they had to pry up a rail and tamp more earth under the ties.

Joe would pronounce approval of a job with, "Dot's pooty goot; leetle rest now." After reloading his pipe and another smoke, Joe's "Shootels on de car," was the signal to load up their tools and move on to the next job or head for their trackside home.

Sometimes a party of Indians would stop and gravely shake hands all around after their gruff but cordial salutation. Once, an old ex-chief, "savage but splendid," stopped at the section house, made a courtly bow, and shook everyone's hand. Then he showed them a rifle that had been given him in earlier days. As they examined it, "he looked on all the while much as a mother might who had consigned her offspring into strange hands."

A small pool near the section house provided their water. When it got difficult to find water without tadpoles, they would load a barrel on their hand car and bring better water from a spring several miles away.

When autumn came, they enjoyed hunting prairie chickens, ducks, and geese. The prairie was alive with gophers and badgers, and occasionally they saw the flashing tails of foxes running away.

At times they would see bands of Indians moving slowly past. The women and babies, along with packs of household goods, rode on the trailing ends of tipi poles drawn by horses. A pack of yelping dogs always brought up the rear.

After the snows came, the frosted rails glistened brightly in the sunshine and seemed to give off cheery rings as the hand car wheels passed over.

Sometimes they were surprised to meet a train, and would have to hurry to get the hand car off the rails before colliding with it. In one close call, they had been ordered out in the evening to unload a train of gravel that was supposed to stop at a certain point. When they saw a light approaching, they pumped their car down to meet the train, but the light didn't stop as they expected.

Joe was frantically shouting, "no poomp, no poomp," as they approached on a slight downgrade. The crew barely had time to leap off from both sides of the hand car before the cowcatcher crashed into it. Their car was splintered and one large piece injured the Irish-Canadian, although not seriously.

The light was not on the train they expected, but on a pay car, long overdue. After the pay car with its indignant paymaster left the accident scene, they piled the pieces of their hand car beside the track, shouldered their shovels, and marched back to the section house, "a crestfallen band." The gravel train arrived the next morning.

Their replacement hand car almost came to grief, also. One breezy morning they were working on a slight downgrade, when someone saw that the wind had started the hand car moving. Running hard, they caught up and got the car off the track just before another train arrived.

The writer said little about recreation. Once, during a three-day rain storm when they couldn't work, they spent time playing cards and reading.

One regular task when the wind permitted was to burn the prairie about sixty feet on each side of the track. This guarded against fires kindled by sparks from passing engines. Joe would move ahead with a burning oil rag on a wire, and the rest of the gang followed. Each man carried an old sack to beat out the fire as it reached its limit.

The writer mentioned mosquitos. If a window was left open, they could not sleep for the "myriad swarms." The large black flies were "voracious, appeasing themselves on our blood."

No whisky could be sold in the region where they worked.

By November, all men except the boss and two on each gang, were released. No more work could be done on the roadbed until the frost broke up in the spring. A train would move down the track toward Winnipeg, stopping to pick up the discharged men along the way.

"A motley crew we were, cooped up together through what seemed an eternity, the only diversion being the passing of the train-boy offering his wares for sale, and the occasional quarreling of the men after the whiskey region had been reached."

So ended another season for a section gang in Canada.

Suggested reading: "Section Life in the North-West" in *The Cornhill Magazine*, London, January, 1888.

WAR IN THE GORGE

Wagon freight for silver from Leadville, Colorado, mines to Cañon City was four cents a pound for the 120-mile haul. Railroad freight for the two thousand mile trip on to New York was less. Both the Denver & Rio Grande, who had laid tracks to Cañon City, and the Santa Fe, whose nearest tracks were at Pueblo, forty-three miles east, had thought about extending track to Leadville to capture that market. But the only place for a railroad west from Cañon City was at the bottom of the Royal Gorge, a thousand feet below the canyon rim. And there was only room for one railroad in that gorge.

On April 10, 1878, the Santa Fe announced that they would build through the gorge. General William J. Palmer, Rio Grande President, immediately sent a coded wire to Chief Engineer J. A. McMurtrie: "Rush a crew to Cañon City and get into the gorge first."

Several years before, McMurtrie, with William R. Morley assisting, had surveyed a line through the gorge, but no drawings had been filed, and the gorge was still open to anyone who took possession.

The Santa Fe intercepted and decoded the Rio Grande wire. Chief Engineer, A. A. Robinson, cabled Morley, who now worked for them, to see if he could beat McMurtrie's crew into the gorge.

Morley reached Pueblo near midnight, April 18, and learned that a large crew of Rio Grande men had already left on a late-night work train to take possession the next morning. Morley hurried to a livery stable, hired a rig and driver, and sped west toward Cañon City.

Morley beat the work train, but he was alone, and he knew the train would have engineers, surveyors, and a grading crew. Then Morley remembered that Cañon City citizens liked the Santa Fe more than the Rio Grande, and one of them, hardware dealer James McClelland, had a stock of tools. He got McClelland to open up, had an earnest conversation with him, took one shovel, and started at a run for the gorge, three miles away.

By the time the Rio Grande crew reached the gorge, McClelland had joined Morley with a hurriedly-raised crew of Cañon City citizens. They were working under Morley's direction when the Rio Grande men arrived.

After hot words and some flourishing of guns, Morley and McMurtrie, — still old friends — got their crews calmed down. But both sides, expecting future trouble, built rock forts at strategic points in the gorge.

Meanwhile, both companies moved the controversy into court. A county judge granted an injunction to the Santa Fe, ordering the Rio Grande men to stop their work. McMurtrie pulled some of his men out, leaving others to man the forts they had built.

That night Morley heard that the Rio Grande crew had received a shipment of guns. He slipped into the baggage room at Cañon City, found the rifles, and removed and hid all their firing pins. But no showdown came, and court orders and writs continued to fly. The press took up the battle, with the *Rocky Mountain News* leading one side, and the *Denver Tribune* the other.

Santa Fe's survey crew reached Leadville in June. But back in the canyon, bridges were being burned, rocks were being pushed over canyon walls, and sections of the newly-made grade were being blown out by blasting powder or buried under tons of rock, dynamited off the canyon walls.

The battle continued in both state and federal courts, first one side winning, then the other. Finally, in March, 1879, the war took a bizarre turn.

Canadian brothers Bat and Ed Masterson, who had moved to Kansas with their parents, had once done some grading for the Santa Fe at Dodge City, Kansas. Then they had turned to buffalo hunting and followed that with careers as famous law officers. On March 20 the Santa Fe cabled the Mastersons that the Rio Grande had recruited professional gunmen for the war, and the railroad needed help. A few days later, the Mastersons arrived with a hundred men armed to the teeth.

The opposing gunmen, wary but quiet, patrolled a month or two and then gradually faded away. They spent more time in Pueblo gambling dens than on the front lines. The court battles continued.

Then in June, a state court judge ordered the Santa Fe to stop operating its trains in Colorado. The railroad again called for Bat Masterson's help. This time his ranks included Ben Thompson, who had been a Texas Ranger and later one of Texas' most spectacular gunmen and gamblers.

Masterson's fifty armed men took possession of the Santa Fe property to protect it from Rio Grande men. In one skirmish a Rio Grande man was killed and another wounded. Then the Rio Grande chief engineer, cooperating with a deputy sheriff, issued rifles and bayonets to his men. Soon a Sante Fe man was killed.

Rather than fight the sheriff's deputies, Masterson returned to Dodge City, and Ben Thompson returned to Austin. The railroad war was over with the victorious Rio Grande in possession of the Royal Gorge. Their first train reached Leadville in July, 1880.

Suggested reading: James Marshall, *Santa Fe* (New York: Random House, 1945).

WHATEVER IS FAIR AND RIGHT

For forty years Fred Harvey did business on a handshake and followed one simple rule. The rule, whether dealing with customers or suppliers, was "whatever is fair and right."

Fifteen-year-old Fred left his London home in 1850 with ten dollars and a ticket from Liverpool to New York. Shortly after reaching the new world, he found work in a Washington street restaurant and bar at two dollars a week. He saved enough to sail on to New Orleans for work in another restaurant. He saved enough there to go upriver to St. Louis and open his own place.

In 1859 Fred married Sally, a seventeen-year-old Bohemian girl from Prague. The Civil War destroyed the restaurant business, and Fred worked on a river boat plying between St. Louis and St. Joseph. Then he worked the mail cars on the Hannibal & St. Joseph Railroad, usually called the Horrible and Slow Jolting.

After Fred and Sally had seven children, five of whom survived infancy, Fred joined the Burlington, rising to Western Freight Agent.

Traveling as freight agent, Fred had his fill of filthy railroad lunch stands serving "railroad pie" and tasteless sandwiches. He tried to interest the Burlington in a cooperative venture to provide decent food for travelers, but the railroad said, "no."

Then Fred went to Charles Morse, whom he had known when Morse worked on the Burlington. Morse, then superintendent of the Santa Fe, liked good food, and he told Fred to go ahead. Fred set up the first Harvey House in Santa Fe's Topeka depot. Then he expanded to a rundown hotel in Florence, a town of one hundred on down the line. This became the first Santa Fe - Fred Harvey hotel and restaurant.

With new furniture, beds, silverware, and cooking equipment, the hotel became a sensation in the small town. But when Fred hired the head chef at Chicago's famous Palmer House at the unheard of salary of five thousand dollars a year, the traveling public really took notice. The chef also became a hero to local farmers, paying unbelievable prices for fresh produce.

Fred and the Santa Fe advertised for waitresses all over the east and middle west. No experience was necessary, but they insisted that the women be young — eighteen to thirty — attractive, intelligent, and of good character. The last requirement was strictly enforced; the girls worked under the stern eye of a matron, slept in dormitories, and had to be in by ten o'clock.

The girls also promised, when hired, to not marry in less than a year, but love usually found its own way. Fred always congratulated a girl who got through six months without an engagement ring, but he also put on regular parties for newlyweds.

The girls had to wear black shoes and stockings and a plain black and white dress with a black bow. They had to wear their hair plain with a simple white ribbon, neatly tied.

The waitresses usually married well, often to Santa Fe engineers, conductors, and station agents. About five thousand of these intelligent and attractive women of good character became wives in the West. A western legend says that about four thousand baby boys born in the West were christened Fred or Harvey or both.

The standard Harvey meal cost fifty cents. You could have a thick steak for breakfast, smothered in eggs, with a side platter of hash brown potatoes. Then came six pan-sized wheat cakes, floating in maple syrup, followed by apple pie and coffee.

Fred Harvey insisted that his patrons be properly dressed, which included coats for the men. Loaner coats were available. Waitresses were ordered to ignore the occasional bore who insisted that his personal freedom prevailed over Fred Harvey's sense of proper attire. The no-coat-no-eat order brought on protracted litigation in Oklahoma. Finally the state supreme court upheld Harvey and chided the chairman of the State Corporation Commission, who had insisted that wearing a coat to dine offended Sooner custom.

A long time Harvey rule allowed a discount to children in highchairs. This sometimes resulted in large, protesting children being stuffed into highchairs by economy-minded parents.

Fred Harvey allowed substitutions, but never varied the advertised price for a meal. In 1897, when the meal was seventy-five cents, a traveler named Jones at La Junta, Colorado, spurned the steak and wanted beans. He got his beans, along with a bill for the listed price - seventy-five cents.

A few hours later the La Junta House paid eighty-five cents for a collect telegram to learn that Mr. Jones hadn't appreciated his bill. Several hours later it paid $2.25 for a collect wire from San Francisco to learn that Mr. Jones still felt that way. Then came a $5.67 collect wire from Mexico City, saying, "I still think you charged me too much for those beans. Jones."

Fred Harvey, a man of principle, paid the charges but refused to alter his rules about substitutions.

Suggested reading: James Marshall, *Santa Fe* (New York: Random House, 1945).

MOSES OF THE MENNONITES

In the last quarter of the nineteenth century western railroads realized their need for settlers. They needed to turn their enormous land subsidies into cash, and they needed new customers to ship supplies in and agricultural and mining produce out.

Many railroad land departments turned to false advertising. They claimed that any easterner, willing to work, could make a good living as a farmer or tradesman. They wanted no lawyers, doctors, clergyman, or others with liberal educations, living by their wits; they had an oversupply of those. But even such blatant lies that incomes in the West would be higher than in the east and cost of living automatically lower failed to produce the needed settlers. So they turned to Europe.

The Chicago, Burlington & Quincy set up an office in Liverpool, England. Their representative handed out pamphlets on every ship crossing the Atlantic, visited all hotels and boarding houses, posted maps in all public buildings showing Burlington's route and available lands, and he published articles in all newspapers read by the "emigrating class." He extolled the salubrious climate in Burlington's territory (Nebraska, Wyoming, and Montana), and often visited large manufacturing towns and agricultural districts throughout England and Scotland to spread his message.

The Northern Pacific had over eight hundred agents in Great Britain and over a hundred more extending from Scandanavia to Switzerland.

The agents soon found that racial or religious groups were their best targets. Ministers in depressed areas were receptive, and their followers tended to believe their advice. After one Swedish minister brought his entire community to Minnesota in 1872, the Northern Pacific put him on commission to return to Sweden and persuade other ministers to bring their congregations.

The Santa Fe hired Carl B. Schmidt, a German-speaking farm-implement dealer in Lawrence, Kansas, to carry their plea to Germany. While there, Schmidt learned about the plight of the Mennonites who had left Germany for Russia in the eighteenth century. Catherine the Great had promised them exemption from compulsory military service, which was against their religion, and assured them they could retain their customs and their language. But in 1870 the Czar canceled the privileges, stating: "One Czar, one religion, one language."

Schmidt, posing as a farm machinery salesman, slipped into Russia and carried his message to people eager to hear it. He said the Kansas plains were better for wheat raising than the Russian steppes, and there were no wild Indians. He said nothing about grasshoppers or drought.

On August 16, 1874, thirty-four Mennonite families from the

Crimea arrived in Kansas. Before leaving, they had quietly converted their property into gold coins, which they sewed into their clothing. Soon afterward, six hundred more Mennonites arrived, and, on September 23, eleven hundred more came, looking for Schmidt, who was then being called the "Moses of the Mennonites."

At first the local Kansans ridiculed the Santa Fe for bringing in these human scarecrows. The men, usually tall and bearded, wore Russian blouses and billowing trousers. But when the locals noticed how the strangers jingled as they walked, rumors soon spread that the Mennonites had brought in two million dollars in gold. The governor had a special reception for them before the Santa Fe started selling land and relieving them of some of their money.

Eventually fifteen thousand Mennonites came to America, practically all from Russia. They brought an extensive knowledge of dryland farming, which they had learned on the arid steppes. They also brought their own Turkey Red wheat, which proved immune to rust and other diseases common to American varieties.

The Mennonites became so desirable as settlers that other railroads tried to steal them. Carl J. Ernst, a Burlington agent, bragged that he stole a whole trainload at once.

A train of Mennonites had arrived in Atchison, where the Santa Fe had a special train waiting. But an empty Burlington train waited nearby, and its agent slipped aboard and led the Mennonites' away.

"I stole the whole bunch," agent Ernst bragged. "We gave them a free ride up to Lincoln on our own special train."

Suggested reading: Dee Brown, *Hear That Lonesome Whistle Blow* (New York: Holt, Rinehart & Winston, 1977).

Mennonite Barracks in Kansas
Leslie's Illustrated Newspaper, March 20, 1875

EMIGRANT TRAIN

In August, 1879, when Robert Louis Stevenson traveled from his native Scotland to California to be with Mrs. Fanny Osbourne, with whom he had fallen in love in France, he wrote a fascinating description of travel on emigrant trains.

After reaching the Missouri River at Council Bluffs, Stevenson and about a hundred others were "sorted and boxed" for the rest of the journey. The three passenger cars on their train were assigned to families (rear car), single men (central), and Chinese (front). There were so many single men that they overflowed into the other two cars. Very likely not many Chinese were traveling west at that time, so designating one car for them was just a means of segregating them from the families. The train also had several freight cars ahead of the Chinese car.

Each car had a stove at one end, a "convenience" at the other, and a passage down the middle, flanked by benches on each side. Each bench would seat two men with little elbow room. The backs were reversible.

When night came, two facing benches could be turned into a sleeping platform for two "amicable" men if they each bought a plank and some small, straw-filled, cushions from the conductor. The conductor introduced likely couples for this nighttime arrangement, sometimes guaranteeing the amiability and honesty of one to a reluctant partner.

Of course, the nighttime capacity of a car was only half what it was during the day. One supposes the men who were excluded (by choice or rejection) from the nighttime arrangement had to curl up on the floor below the paired ones, sleeping above. Not allowed in the family car, Stevenson does not tell how the chilren were probably shoved into every nook or cavern possible to make room for their parents to sleep side by side.

With a thunderstorm outside and a cornet-playing passenger inside, Stevenson's first evening aboard was a restless one. The cornet player was a nuisance until he started "Home, Sweet Home." Then, as tears began to fill some eyes, an elderly, hard-looking man growled, "Stop that damned thing. We've heard enough of that. Give us something about the good country we're going to."

The passengers could not predict their arrival time in California closer than one or two days, as the emigrant train gave way to all other traffic on the railway. Their first twenty-four hours brought them about two hundred seventy-five miles to North Platte.

During their first day in Nebraska, Stevenson rode on top of a freight car. The world seemed featureless to him, an empty sky, an empty earth, with the railroad tracks stretching from horizon to horizon. Wild sunflowers made a continuous flower-bed, and buffalo grazed in the distance. Day and night, above the sound of the steam-driven engine, they could hear the incessant chirping of grasshoppers. Now and then distant dots would grow into cabins, only to disappear in the train's wake as it moved on across the barren land.

As they "hurried" along, Stevenson thought of "the old days" with men plodding along beside slow-moving oxen.

The conductor hardly talked to the passengers after he had sold them their bed boards and cushions. He would not even answer simple questions, apparently considering the emigrants as less than human. They had to rely on the newsboy for information about the country they passed through.

Their first newsboy was an insolent scoundrel who treated them with contempt. But the one they had from Ogden to Sacramento was friendly, telling the emigrants where they should eat, how long the train would stop, and watching that they were not left behind.

Conductors did not call "All Aboard" when leaving a station as they did on other trains. The emigrant train would steal from the station without a word of warning, requiring its passengers to keep a watchful eye while they ate. One suspects that the families brought their own food, but apparently the single men ate in stations along the way.

After the dreary Nebraska plains, Stevenson looked forward to crossing the high plains and mountains of Wyoming. He was disappointed. As they traveled through one sterile canyon after another, he thought the train was the one live thing in "a deadly land."

The night Stevenson left Laramie was one he could not forget. The sleepers lay in uneasy positions, "here two chums alongside, flat upon their backs like dead folk; there a man sprawling on the floor, with his face upon his arm; there another half-seated with his head and shoulders upon the bench.

"The most passive were continually and roughly shaken by the movement of the train; others stirred, turned, or stretched out their arms like children; it was surprising how many groaned and murmured in their sleep; and as I passed to and fro, stepping across the prostrate, and caught now a snore, now a gasp, now a half-formed word, it gave me a measure of the worthlessness of rest in that unresting vehicle. Although it was chill, I was obliged to open my window, for the degradation of the air soon became intolerable."

At Ogden he was glad to change from the Union Pacific to the Central Pacific. The cars in which they had ridden for ninety hours were stinking unbearably. He noted that the Chinese car was the least offensive, and the one containing the women and children smelled the worst.

The Central Pacific cars were nearly twice as high and much airier. They gave the passengers a sense of cleanliness as though they had bathed.

The seats could be pulled toward the aisle and joined, so the passengers no longer needed bed boards. There was an upper tier of berths which could be closed by day and opened at night.

But Stevenson could not sleep in his upper berth. The air, bad enough at floor level, was so foul immediately under the roof, that sleep was impossible. Shut into a "kind of Saratoga trunk with one side partly open," the attempt to sleep was madness.

"Though the fumes were narcotic and weighed upon the eyelids, yet they so smartly irritated the lungs that I could only lie and cough. I spent the better part of one night walking to and fro and envying my neighbors."

Stevenson unfavorably contrasted the emigrants traveling to the West with those who had crossed the Atlantic. "They were mostly lumpish fellows, silent and noisy, a common combination; somewhat sad I should say, with an extraordinary poor taste in humour, and little interest in their fellow-creatures beyond that of a cheap and merely external curiosity. If they heard a man's name and business, they seemed to think they had the heart of the mystery; but they were as eager to know that much as they were indifferent to the rest."

Utah and Nevada did not impress Stevenson. But he awoke as they traveled down through a succession of snow sheds. Between these dark tunnels they saw pine forests, a foaming river, and a sky "coloured with the fires of dawn."

Stevenson knew he had "come home again — home from unsightly deserts to the green and habitable corners of the earth."

The passengers bawled like schoolboys as they feasted their eyes on "the good country they had been going to so long." Soon they would leave the train for their new homes.

Suggested reading: Robert Louis Stevenson, "Across the Plains" in *From Scotland to Silverado* (Cambridge: Harvard University Press, 1966).

SECTION HOUSE MOTHER

Margaret Flannigan was eleven when her mother died, leaving Margaret in charge of household duties for her father and three younger brothers. John and Mary Flannagan had immigrated from Ireland to Scranton, Pennsylvania, and John worked in the mines there.

Four years later, in 1877, John moved his family to Jamestown, Dakota Territory, to work on the Northern Pacific Railroad. Jamestown was just a fort and a town of a few tents. The Flannigans lived in a section house for a year, and then John was transferred thirty-five miles west to become section foreman at Crystal Springs. They spent five years in Crystal Springs, living in the section house there.

No schooling or church services were available in Crystal Springs. The children enjoyed meeting every train crew and talking to them. The crews brought them their food and any clothing they might need from Jamestown. Snowstorms and blizzards were their greatest amusement. The boys enjoyed hunting and fishing. Antelope and buffalo were plentiful, and fresh meat was abundant in the Flannagan home.

John Flannagan worried that Crystal Springs was too isolated and lonely for his children, so he arranged for a transfer to Terry, Montana, in 1883. Margaret was now twenty-one.

The section house was the only building in Terry. The people, mostly Indians and cowboys, were a wild lot, but friendly. All that came to Terry camped around the section house, but the Flannagans never had trouble with them. Margaret could see buffalo herds from the house, and her father and brothers brought much fresh meat for her to cook.

Three years later, the family returned to Jamestown, where Margaret met and married George Gates, a young man from Minnesota who had come West for adventure. He had been a teamster on a mail route from Bismarck to the Black Hills, and later a fireman on the railroad.

When she was seventy-six, Margaret told the field worker taking her history that she enjoyed visiting her grown children, one week at a time. She and George had had six children, including two sets of twins, one set of which died in infancy. Margaret said she would have been glad to live the same life over again.

Suggested reading: Elizabeth Hampsten, *Settlers' Children* (Norman: University of Oklahoma Press, 1991).

CENTRAL PACIFIC NO. ONE

The first train robbed in the West was Central Pacific No. One, an eastbound express. The date was November 5, 1870, and the place was Verdi, Nevada, a few miles east of the California line. In fact, before the day was over and before the train got out of Nevada, it became the second train robbed in the West. If they gave medals to robbed trains, the double-barreled attack would have given Central Pacific No. One both gold and silver.

The express — a baggage car, day coach, and sleeper — pulled out of Oakland on November 4 behind its red, wood-burning engine and had an easy run until it reached the Sierra foothills.

The climb over the mountains was uneventful until the train reached a lumber siding at Verdi, Nevada. Then six masked men ran out from the shadows in bright moonlight and jumped aboard.

When conductor Mitchell saw the rough-looking men with handguns instead of tickets, he thought they just wanted to steal rides. But the engineer, a gun in his ribs, had been ordered to proceed slowly with the baggage car, dropping the remainder of the train behind. He signaled the brakeman at the rear, and swift hands unhooked the passenger cars from the baggage car and engine. When Mitchell stepped to the ground, he saw the business half of the train receding in the distance.

Wells Fargo Messenger Frank Marshall, alone in the baggage car with a heavy shipment of gold and silver, expected a stop at Reno to put off the gold. But when the train stopped at an abandoned stone quarry about six miles east of Verdi and Marshall opened the door, he saw six masked strangers, not the Reno Wells Fargo agent.

The masked men threw the engineer and fireman into the baggage car and forcibly removed over forty thousand dollars worth of gold and coins. They passed up the silver bars, deciding they were too heavy to carry. Then the men disappeared into the desert, some of them carrying coins in old boots, used as grip bags.

Meanwhile, conductor Mitchell, realizing that he lacked an engine but had downhill tracks, ordered the brakeman to release the brakes. Just as the engineer and fireman were thinking about backing up to recover the missing cars, they saw the cars approaching. The reunited train went on to Reno and telegraphed to the world that something new had been added to western railroading.

With a new crew aboard, Number One chugged on northeast toward its second rendezvous with trouble. At eleven fifteen that night it pulled out of Independence, the third siding east of Wells in the Pequop Mountains of Nevada. By now the full moon was covered with clouds; the shadows were not as sharp as they had been earlier.

Suddenly four men ran out from an old shed to jump aboard, two on the engine and two on the baggage car. These men carried rifles and carbines in addition to revolvers. Although there was no connection between the two bands of robbers, the second group also detached the passenger part of the train containing the conductor, brakeman, and passengers.

Six miles down the road — an upgrade at that place — the severed cars were far behind. The robbers threw off the fireman, mail clerk, and messenger and told the engineer — rifle at his neck — to keep going.

Near the Pequop siding the train was halted. The robbers, finding the treasure pretty well picked over, still got a silver bar, fourteen hundred dollars in coin, twenty-six hundred dollars in dust, and twenty-three packages of mail. Then they jumped on their waiting horses, and disappeared.

Conductor Carter on the relief crew had listened to passengers brag about how things would have been different if THEY had been aboard the earlier train. When his cars were detached, he told the passengers they now had their chance. Many passenger sidearms mysteriously disappeared or became suddenly disfunctional.

But a small volunteer posse did charge out into the night, searching for the robbers. What they found was the business half of the train, backing down to again pick up its rear half. Then the train continued on east. Pursuers on both of Nevada's western and eastern borders now searched for two sets of train robbers.

Back in the west, the law moved quickly. About the time the eastern bandits were swinging into action, three men showed up at N. Pearson's tavern northwest of Verdi. One, John Squires, came alone. Shortly after, the other two, E. B. Parsons and Jim Gilchrist, showed up together. They all asked for supper and lodging.

Mrs. Pearson, a curious woman, noticed that the travelers all seemed to know each other. She had heard the news of the robbery and she watched closely.

After breakfast, Squires and Parsons, who had pretended to be strangers the night before, checked out and rode north together. Then a deputy sheriff and a Wells Fargo agent arrived with questions. Mrs. Pearson mentioned the two men riding north. The lawmen followed.

Mrs. Pearson continued to watch Gilchrist. As soon as the lawmen were out of sight, he went to the outhouse behind the tavern. Mrs. Pearson, her curiosity overcoming any modesty, slipped around to peek through a knothole. She saw Gilchrist lower a boot filled with ten thousand dollars in twenty-dollar gold pieces into a convenient hiding place.

Shortly after Gilchrist returned to the tavern, he saw Mr. Pearson stroll down to the outhouse. A little later, Gilchrist looked again for his cache. It was gone.

Pearson ran for a sheriff, who was not hard to find in the area that morning. In fact, Washoe County Undersheriff James Kinkead had already found the place in the stone quarry where the robbers had divided most of their loot. A heel mark there led him on, and he was near Pearson's tavern when Pearson came looking for an officer.

They found Gilchrist in Pearson's barn, but his boots weren't the ones Kinkead had been following. After sending a deputy back with Gilchrist, Kinkead followed tracks in the snow to Loyalton, California, about fifteen miles away. Slipping into a tavern room, recently rented to a stranger, Kinkead extracted a revolver from under the pillow. Then he woke the stranger up. It was Parsons, and the boots matched the print.

With Parsons secured in a dependable saloon, Kinkead pushed on through a winter gale and darkness to Sierraville, twelve miles farther. There he found John Squires at the fugitive's brother's farm. Without a thought about a Nevada officer making arrests in California, Kinkead collared his suspects and took them to Reno.

The other three robbers, plus the man in San Francisco who had tipped them off on what the train was carrying, were also soon arrested. One of the six went free for testifying for the state. The others went to prison.

The eastern band of robbers presented no challenge. Two of them, wearing army uniforms, were identified as deserters from nearby Camp Halleck. Another left a glove, bearing his name, at the scene.

Four posses with special engines and a company of cavalry from Camp Halleck followed a trail of newly-minted half-dollars until the band was sighted south of Great Salt Lake. One pair was captured on the open range; the other was chased into the hands of Mormon authorities.

Central Pacific Number One kept on chugging. For one night in Nevada it had been train of destiny.

Suggested reading: Neill C. Wilson, *Treasure Express* (New York: The Macmillan Company, 1936).

CENTRAL PACIFIC NO. 1
Nevada Historical Society

BILL CRUSH'S KATY CRUSH IN CRUSH, TEXAS

W hen Bill Crush was hired as general passenger agent for the Katy Railroad in 1896, president Henry Rouse said the line needed publicity. Crush, a friend of P. T. Barnum with his own experience in stunts, thought up a good one. He would stage a head-on train crash, bring ticket-buying spectators in excursion trains to view it, and make a ton of money while they let the world know that the main line of the Missouri, Kansas and Texas was now complete from Franklin, Missouri, to Galveston, Texas.

Rouse and the directors had doubts, but Crush argued them away. He selected a shallow, natural amphitheater near West, Texas, a few miles north of Waco. A special siding was built with twenty-one hundred feet of viewing stands. Two outmoded engines — each a 35-ton, diamond stacked, 4-4-0 — were gaudily painted and brought down from Missouri. Each would pull six box cars loaded with ties into a head-on collision at sixty miles per hour.

People paid attention to Crush's nation-wide advertising. September 15 was selected for the crash. Even the intense political campaign of William Jennings Bryan, the Great Commoner, making the first of his three runs for the presidency, went on the back burner.

Rouse worried about spectator safety. Crush said they would pry up a rail behind each train after it started forward. Then if one derailed, the other could not run wild out of the little valley and cause damage. "How about pickpockets?" asked Rouse.

Crush hired two hundred special constables to handle the crowd and built a large, temporary jail for pickpockets and rowdies.

Dozens of excursion trains deposited over thirty-three thousand eager spectators, while locals arrived on horseback and in buggies, all paying two dollars each to see the monster attraction. A large Ringling Brothers circus tent shaded the dining area here Katy cooks served food. Smaller tents were used to dispense lemonade.

Eight tank cars brought drinking water from Waco. Of course, some brought their own drinks in smaller containers. Bands, a midway, and a medicine show entertained as the crowd assembled.

At last Crush signaled the two locomotives to move forward slowly. Like boxers touching gloves at the beginning of a fight, they gently let their cowcatchers touch. Then each backed away a mile and waited for the final signal to rush forward.

But the unruly crowd pushed forward for better views, and it was late afternoon before the constables had sufficient control that Crush could go ahead with his spectacular entertainment.

Crush flashed the signal, and the old trains started forward. Careful practice runs had shown exactly how the throttles should be opened, and how many exhaust strokes should be counted before moving to the final notch (just short of full throttle) when the engineer and fireman would bail out. They had advertised a sixty-mile speed for each engine, a closing speed of one hundred twenty miles an hour.

A thousand torpedoes, carefully set along the track, exploded in turn as the trains approached at increasing speeds. Everything worked perfectly, and the impact came right in front of the grandstand.

Waco photographer Jervis Deane occupied a specially-built platform only a hundred feet from the point of collision. Crush thought pictures of the impact would sell well. Thirteen-year-old Ernest Darnall sat in a nearby mesquite tree so he could have a good view.

Each train's tender and three front boxcars telescoped into the engine, becoming a mass of twisted metal. But no one had anticipated that the boilers would explode. They both blew up together, and loose metal, bolts, and chunks of chain and shrapnel flew in all directions.

A piece of chain split Ernest Darnall's skull, killing him instantly. Another boy had a jagged hole ripped into his leg by a flying bolt. Another bolt gouged Jervis Deane's eye out, just after he got his successful picture. DeWitt Barnes stood between his wife and another woman. They were untouched, but he was killed instantly, his head nearly torn off by a flying chunk of metal.

In spite of two dead and several seriously wounded, the crowd rushed forward to collect souvenirs from the steaming mass of metal lying before them.

The temporary town, well-named Crush, Texas, only lasted a day or two. Katy trains still go through the shallow valley. Nearby West is not much bigger than it was then. Perhaps some train passengers imagine they can hear today the screaming chunks of metal that turned a gigantic publicity stunt into a bloody disaster for a few spectators.

Scott Joplin composed a song, The Great Crush Collision March, to honor the event. Now the world had heard about the Katy Railroad!

Suggested reading: Nancy M. Peterson, "Wreck and Ruin on the Katy" in *True West* (July, 1999).

MOUNTAIN RUNAWAY

Shortly after midnight on January 20, 1883, the Southern Pacific's *Overland Express* en route from San Francisco to Los Angeles, stopped at the foot of the Tehachapi Mountains to pick up its helper engine. The train had to climb thirteen hundred feet in twenty-eight miles of track to reach the summit. Normally the helper engine would hook on in front of the regular engine, so it could easily be unhooked at the summit. No one knows why, but on this night the helper was hooked in between the regular engine and the first baggage car.

Behind the helper were two baggage cars and the mail express. Then came two pullman cars, a smoker, and a coach at the rear. Between sixty and seventy persons were aboard. They included twenty Chinese track laborers in the smoker and about the same number of passengers in the coach.

John G. Downey, former California governor, and his wife were aboard. Mrs. Downey was deathly afraid of trains. At one time, she swore she would never ride another one. Only her husband's heart-felt plea and the fact that they were returning home to Los Angeles got her on this one.

The night was windy and bitterly cold. A few nights before, it had been twenty degrees below zero at the summit. Two and a half hours were required to reach Tehachapi Station at the top of the pass. The cars were warm and stuffy from coal stoves. Most of the passengers were asleep when the train stopped.

Passenger G. H. McKenzie, a former brakeman, could not sleep. He had been talking with the conductor near the front of the smoker when the conductor stepped off to check in at the station. McKenzie then moved out to the smoker platform for some fresh air.

The forward brakeman was helping uncouple the helper engine so it could head back down the track. McKenzie was surprised to see the rear brakeman walk past, escorting a young woman passenger to the station. McKenzie remembered from his experience that a brakeman was never supposed to leave his train. The rear brakeman soon reappeared, but the wind blew his lantern out, and he returned to the station to light it.

Then McKenzie felt the cars moving slowly backward. He thought they were backing into a siding. But when they passed the siding and McKenzie saw they were still on the main track, he grew alarmed. He gripped the handrail and leaned out as far as he could to see the front end of the train. There was no engine there!

McKenzie leaped for the hand-brake wheel on the platform of the smoker. It would not budge. He jumped to the rear platform of the adjacent pullman. He could turn that wheel slightly, but it had no effect on the train. McKenzie, desperate, yelled for help and dashed through the smoker to its rear platform. He could make that brake take hold, but the train was now rolling at a frightening speed.

The cars rocked and swayed dizzily, reeling around curves. By now, another passenger was helping McKenzie, so he ran back to the front platform and tried that brake wheel again. As the train screeched around a curve, the coupling between the smoker and the pullman ahead of it broke. The uphill part of the train cascaded off the track into a crunching heap. The thunder of its destruction woke ranchers in the mountains.

The smoker and coach, still hitched together, continued racing downhill. Passengers struggled mightily on all four of the hand brakes. After two more miles of travel, they forced the cars to a stop. They looked up the mountain and saw the flames from the derailed cars.

McKenzie ordered some men to stay behind with the women and children. The rest followed him up the track to see what they could do.

There had been some heroic rescues. But by the time the coach and smoker passengers got there, the flames had consumed all who were not thrown free or pulled from the wreckage.

Governor Downey had been pulled out, nearly strangled. His wife, along with twelve other passengers, were dead. Two more injured passengers died within a few days.

Suggested reading: Wesley S. Griswold, *Train Wreck*! Brattleboro: The Stephen Greene Press, 1969).

Tehachapi Wreck on January 20, 1883
Leslie's Illustrated Newspaper, Feb. 3, 1883

A LEGEND OF COURAGE

Fifteen-year-old Kate Shelley loved the railroad. A plain-faced, stocky girl, deeply religious, she was used to hard work. Her father, an Irish immigrant from Tipperary who had become a section foreman on the Chicago & Northwestern, had been dead for three years. His widow and five children stayed on in their small cottage beside Honey Creek near Boone, Iowa. The C&NW main line ran close by, and Kate knew all the train crews.

On July 6, 1881, the rain began in early afternoon. By dark it was falling in torrents, with Honey Creek nearing flood stage. When Kate saw their barn in danger, she fought her way through cascades of water to open the doors, letting the horses and cows escape to higher ground. She wrapped two baby pigs in her apron and brought them to the kitchen.

Kate and her mother sat up to watch the storm, while the smaller children slept fitfully. Between lightning flashes they saw boards, fenceposts and uprooted trees tumbling down Honey Creek. The rising water turned their yard into a treacherous lake. They wondered how long the railroad bridge over the creek and the longer wooden trestle over the Des Moines River, a half mile away, could stand the onslaught.

Shortly after eleven, they heard the approach of the helper engine that was stationed in Moingona to push heavy freights up the grade from the Des Moines River. The engine, running light, was backing down to the Honey Creek bridge. Kate saw the bridge swing crazily, and then the engine light suddenly disappeared.

"Oh mother," Kate screamed. "The pusher's gone down."

They heard the crash and the hiss of escaping steam above the roar of the storm. Kate jumped up and grabbed her coat.

"The crew will need help," she said. "And the midnight express! They won't know the bridge is out."

"Go then in the name of God, and do what you can," her mother said.

Kate grabbed an old lantern and ran from the house. The other children, awakened by Kate's scream, watched, their faces drawn and pale.

When Kate reached the bridge, she saw that Ed Wood, the engineer, and Adam Agar, the brakeman, had pulled themselves up into some trees and were safe for the time being from the maelstrom of churning water at their feet. They knew nothing about the fireman or the section boss. Kate shouted that she would try to reach Moingona to warn the station about the bridge.

When she reached the long trestle over the Des Moines River, the storm's fury had increased. Thunder shook the earth, and the jagged lightning, almost continuous now, had turned the sky into a cauldron of unearthly lights.

Rain pelted Kate's small body like hail stones. She knew that the trestle, already weakened by earlier rains, would be dangerous with the rush of water and debris shaking it so furiously. Yet, if she didn't warn the train it would surely crash through the trestle or the downed bridge, bringing death to hundreds. She breathed a prayer through trembling lips and crawled out on the first ties of the 500-foot trestle.

Kate's lantern had already blown out from the gale-strength winds. She would have to crawl on hands and knees on the ties, clutching a rail for support, with only the lightning to show the way.

Kate's knees slipped on the rain-soaked ties. From time to time her skirt caught on a spike, nearly pitching her into the chaos just below. The spikes and splinters tore at her hands and knees. Every moment she feared that she might suddenly see the headlight of the doomed train.

Halfway across she saw a huge tree, its matted roots bearing down like a battering ram in the raging torrent. Somehow it slipped between two piers, spraying Kate with leaves and mud. Muttering a prayer of thanks, the trembling girl continued on. Her bloodied hands slipped when she had to grip new spikes, and her strength began to ebb. The wind seemed to be trying to tear her from the trestle, and she wondered if she would ever reach the end.

After a time of terror that she could not even estimate, Kate finally felt the wet earth, and she knew she was safely across. Moingona was still a half mile away. She ran the whole distance, and staggered into the station, wild eyed and mud-smeared.

The station master, thinking she was deranged, refused to listen to her. But another railroad man recognized Mike Shelley's daughter.

"It's Kate Shelley," he said. "Child what brings you forth in this storm?"

"The bridge is down," Kate sobbed. "Stop the express! And Wood and Agar are hanging in a tree. You must go get them."

Then the whistle sounded on the approaching express. The station master ordered the signal, and the train ground to a halt, a trainload of people saved from death or injury.

The crew uncoupled the engine and went on ahead to rescue the helper engine crew. Kate went with them, going out on the trestle for the second time that storm-wracked night.

They got the engineer that night, the brakeman the next day. They found the section foreman's body downstream. The fireman's body was never found.

Kate Shelley became a national hero. Poems, songs, and stories were written to celebrate the girl's courage and endurance. Letters came from all over the world, some asking for bits of Kate's dress or splinters from the bridge as souvenirs. The Iowa legislature gave her a gold medal. The school children of Dubuque raised money for another medal. The *Chicago Tribune* raised funds to help the Shelleys get out of debt.

A scholarship fund was raised so Kate could go to college. She started two years later, when she finished high school. But she was needed at home and she found college difficult, so she dropped out after one year.

In 1886, the Brotherhood of Railroad Trainmen organized the Boone local. It is named for Kate, the only railroad brotherhood lodge named for a woman.

The Chicago & Northwestern gave Kate a lifetime pass. When the railroad rebuilt the line twenty years later, the new iron bridge across the Des Moines River was named the Kate Shelley Bridge. In the 1950s the railroad named a new passenger train, THE KATE SHELLEY 400 in honor of her memory.

Kate's health was never good after the memorable night when she saved the train. She never married. In 1903 she became station agent at Moingona, a position she held until her death in 1912.

In 1956 the Order of Railway Conductors and Brakemen placed a plaque on Kate's grave in Boone. It reads:

Here's a deed for legends, a story to be told until the last order fades, the last rail rusts.

Suggested reading: Freeman H. Hubbard, *Railroad Avenue* (New York: McGraw Hill Book Co., Inc., 1945).

TUNES ALONG LAKE FORK

On August 15, 1889, the Denver & Rio Grande dispatched its first train on a new, 36-mile branch line from Sapinero, Colorado, up the Lake Fork of the Gunnison River to Lake City. The branch line had made Lake City the shipping point for gold and silver ore and for cattle and other agricultural production.

Lake City was the seat of a county larger than Rhode Island, but with few people. The continental divide crossed it twice, so the northern and southern portions were on the Pacific side, while the central portion drained to the Atlantic. Many of its few hundred citizens were isolated from their county seat all winter by deep snow.

For the next thirty-two years the railroad ran daily trains up the Lake Fork and back. Most of them had only two cars behind the engine, the tender and a combination car for passengers and freight. But during all those thirty-two years, it had only one engineer, Pete Ready.

Passengers in both Sapinero and Lake City grew accustomed to hearing the conductor shouting from the rear, "Ready, Pete?" The engineer, just a short distance ahead, would respond, "Nope, I'm Pete Ready." Then the gloved fist would open the throttle for yet another trip through the canyons of Lake Fork.

Pete, a Missourian, was thirty-one when he made the first run to Lake City. When he left the run, he had spent more than half his lifetime on it. He soon had the reputation of knowing every spike and tie on the line. He never had a serious accident, a remarkable record for mountain railroading.

Once in November, 1893, as Pete approached Elk Creek, his keen eyes saw roadbed damage ahead. After a spark-showering abrupt stop, he saw that part of the road bed had been washed out, and the tracks swung unsupported over the creek below. Had he not stopped in time, the engine, tender, and car would have plunged to the roiling water below.

Pete not only had a great service record on the Denver & Rio Grande Railroad, he also earned a lasting place in the hearts of the people in Lake Fork Valley. Mrs. Carl Benson lived on a ranch and often flagged the train down to deliver packages of vegetables, butter, cream, and eggs to friends in Lake City. After one such stop she told Pete she wanted to send a dozen eggs to Mrs. Meyers, but only had eleven.

"But a hen's on the nest right now," she said. "Maybe you could wait a little bit and I'll have the full dozen."

Good natured Pete Ready waited, the hen came through, and Mrs. Meyers was not disappointed. Where else did a railroad provide service like that?

Perhaps wanting to bring joy to a region that a few years before had been shocked with Alferd Packer's ghastly cannibalism, Pete learned to play tunes with his train whistle. At least he could get the rhythm, if not the melody, and the residents learned to recognize Pete's artistic productions. Yankee Doodle was his favorite, and he always announced his approach to Lake City with that or a similar "tune." After the company provided him with a new whistle, Pete rose to the opportunity. He soon had an extensive repertory.

As he approached Lake City one day, Pete outdid himself with numbers ranging from Yankee Doodle to old, favorite hymns. By the time the train reached the long bridge at the edge of town, Pete did not have enough steam left to bring the train into the station. The train had to wait a half hour, while Fireman Palmer shoveled coal to build the steam back up. He reportedly told Pete that any repetition would mean Pete would have to fire his own engine.

One day, as Pete whistled his way into the Lake City station, he looked back so he could properly position the coach part of the combination car for loading passengers. To his amazement, the car was missing! He opened the throttle and began backing down the track in search of his train.

Seven miles below town a steep grade ran from High Bridge up to Stony Gulch. Somehow the combination car had come loose from the tender on that grade and had rolled back down, as Pete, unaware, chugged on up the track.

Fortunately the brakeman was able to tighten the hand brake enough to stop the car, but he was relieved to see the engine backing down toward him. Pete coupled to the car and went back to Lake City without incident. But for months afterward friends in Lake City would greet Pete with, "Hey, Pete. Where's your train?"

The branch to Lake City lost its good luck charm when Pete left after thirty-two years to take a passenger run between Montrose and Grand Junction. Plagued by a series of floods, accidents, and low revenue, the branch was closed twelve years later.

Suggested reading: Walter R. Borneman, "Railroading Along Lake Fork," in *Frontier Times* (November, 1977).

LAKE FORK BRANCH - Denver & Rio Grande Western
Colorado Historical Society

GOLD TRAIN

Charles Foster, United States Secretary of the Treasury, got some shocking news in July, 1892. The subtreasury in New York was almost out of gold!

Normally it was not hard to keep gold reserves balanced between subtreasury offices, but the times were not normal. A rash of cashing gold certificates in the east, heavy shipments abroad, and a sluggish economy had created the urgency. If banking houses began to falter, the demand for gold would be enormous. Failing to meet that demand could bring down the nation! Foster pondered what to do.

There was plenty of gold in the San Francisco subtreasury, but how could it be moved quickly to New York? Railway express was not the answer. Robbers often held up trains, concentrating on the express cars in which Wells Fargo and other companies shipped their gold. The bandits carefully avoided the mail cars, because robbing the mail was a federal offense with severe consequences. In fact, during an 1887 robbery on the Missouri Pacific in Texas, the bandits were handed a sack of mail by the express agent. They refused to take it, saying they did not want to rob the mails.

Foster selected James E. White, career postal official and superintendent of the Railway Mail Service, to handle the job. If it could be done, Jim White could do it.

But the job was staggering! It was customary to ship up to $200,000 in gold coin by registered mail, but twenty million was required now! White briefly considered the usual procedure, shipping a million each day instead of $200,000. Twenty successive daily shipments would be required. But knowing that word would leak out if he made that decision and fearing successive holdups, White decided that something else would have to be tried.

White selected five trusted division superintendents, and each of them picked nine of his most loyal and able mail clerks. Preference went to men who had seen combat in the Civil War or on the Indian frontier.

To cover for forty-five railway mail service employees suddenly traveling to California, White made up a story about a new incentive training program. The superintendents were told the task, but the men were kept in the dark until August 4, when they were taken into the San Francisco subtreasury to watch the opening of an army shipment of sixty Springfield carbines and fifty-one Colt revolvers.

The gold was packed into five hundred wooden boxes, each containing 160 pounds. The boxes were divided evenly between four revenue cars. A fifth car, a passenger observation car with a glass front end, was hooked on in front of the revenue cars immediately behind the tender. This eliminated the blind area which had allowed past robbers to jump aboard and reach the engine unseen.

Nine clerk-guards and one superintendent were assigned to each of the five cars — the four revenue cars and the observation car. The men in each car were divided into two five-man squads, so that one squad was wide awake at all times. On-duty men had to sit on chairs near doors or windows with their revolvers holstered and their carbines within reach. An off-duty man could sleep provided his carbine was at his side, the barrel resting against the inside curve of his arm, and his revolver was also within reach.

White held his breath as the heavy cars rolled out of Oakland, heading northeast on Central Pacific tracks toward Sacramento. It would be necessary for four different railway companies to take charge of the train before it reached New York. Had he thought of everything?

"I'm worried about the weight," the engineer had said. "The strain on the cars may be too much."

The engineer was right. An inspection in Sacramento revealed that the drawhead (the frame to which the coupler was attached) on one of the cars had loosened. It was soon fixed and safety chains were installed between the cars. But what about the added stress in crossing the Sierras and the Rockies? A car pulling loose there would be a disaster. No one knew if the newly-designed Westinghouse air brakes would hold a heavily-loaded runaway car.

White listened to the engine strain as it climbed the Sierras. Suddenly, with a frightening jolt, the coupler in the command car gave way! The men held their breath, expecting the cars to come to a stop and then, after a terrifying second of no movement, to start backward, careening out of control on the first fatal curve. But the safety chain jerked and the cars continued up the grade. The train was still intact!

A few miles on, a second coupler broke. After another anxious second, that safety chain held, and the train moved on toward Colfax where repairs could be made.

Then they all heard a loud explosion. Was it dynamite? Was someone trying to blow up the train? The guards rushed to the windows with their guns, ready to defend the train. It was a torpedo, a signal to stop the train. Could it have been planted by robbers? The guards scanned the steep slopes, wondering if armed bandits were about to descend. The work crew — an ordinary section gang — was a beautiful sight with its picks and shovels.

The men relaxed and so did White, seeing that the men had reacted well to the emergencies. After two hours of repairs in Colfax, the train moved on.

White was stunned when they reached Salt Lake City and he saw the newspaper headline: A gigantic shipment of gold was moving from San Francisco to New York!

They had crossed the Sierras and the desert, but the Wyoming Rockies were ideal bandit country. To make matters worse, they got a new engineer at Rawlins and when he learned what the train was carrying, he refused to go. He said he had been held up too many times. White got the division superintendent to find another engineer, and the train continued on its way.

A new excitement emerged as the train waited on a siding near Cheyenne. The guards in the second car heard it first. A low sound of voices and the shuffling of feet from near the forward car. Then the men in the command car heard it. It sounded like it might have been the brakeman, but he had already examined the couplers and drawheads. Whoever it was spoke so softly they obviously didn't want to be heard as they shuffled to the rear.

White motioned the forward car guards into position. Then one kicked open the door and the rest swung into position, their guns leveled. White had warned them to not fire toward the second car, regardless of what they saw outside.

Hearing the commotion, the guards in the second car took the same action. Two ragged tramps, their eyes wide with fright watched as the doors were kicked open and the guns of what seemed like a small army were trained on them! The guards sent the tramps away, and the train moved on into Nebraska.

The engine needed repairs on an eccentric when it reached Omaha. A series of hot boxes had to be fixed in Illinois. Then the train was side-tracked for one carrying Knights of Templars to a convention in Denver.

But that was the last delay. From Chicago they rolled east on the Lake Shore & Michigan Southern. They switched to the New York Central at Buffalo. As the train rolled down the beautiful Hudson River Valley, James White and all of his special crew were thankful they had been spared by a kind Providence throughout the tense journey.

Forty tons of gold — twenty million dollars worth in all — had been shipped safely from coast to coast on one overloaded train guarded by fifty tense railway mail service employees.

Suggested reading: Richard Patterson, *Train Robbery* (Boulder: Johnson Books, 1981).

THE GREAT HINCKLEY FIRE

When the northbound *Duluth Limited* stopped at Hinckley, Minnesota — sixty-five miles north of St. Paul — at two p. m. on September 1, 1894, the twelve hundred residents weren't very worried about the forest fire outside their town. Mostly lumber mill workers, they had seen hazy skies and smelled burning timber before. But forty minutes later when the Eastern Minnesota freight pulled in, the smoke curtain from the walls of flame was closing in from the west, south, and east, the sky had turned dark, and the roaring flames had reached the western outskirts of town.

Two railway lines crossed at Hinckley. The St. Paul and Duluth (later Northern Pacific) ran north and south, and the Eastern Minnesota (later Great Northern) northeast and southwest from St. Cloud to Duluth.

The slow freight had ten loaded cars and thirty empties. An Eastern Minnesota passenger train followed the freight in at three twenty-five, and the two crews made up a combination special of two locomotives, five coaches, three boxcars, and the caboose. They told the residents they would take on all the people who wanted to leave. They would back out to the northeast, away from the fire.

It took forty-five minutes to get the stragglers aboard. By then people and animals were keeling over dead in the streets from the heat. The cars were blistering and smoldering as the train backed out of town, and some ties in the roadbed were on fire. Flames beat against both engine cabs as the engineers opened their throttles. When they reached Sandstone, eight miles away, they were ahead of the fire. Most of those residents declined to get on the crowded train.

They stopped at Partridge long enough that the passengers — many suffering from thirst — could drink all the water they wanted. But there, as well as in Mansfield and Kerrick, the locals refused to desert their town for the overcrowded train.

When the train reached West Superior, Ed Barry, engineer in the lead engine, collapsed and was carried to the hospital.

In the meantime, the southbound *Duluth Limited*, with young engineer James Root on the throttle and Jack McGowan shoveling coal, reached Hinckley a few minutes after the Eastern Minnesota train backed out. People were running frantically toward the train, and Root brought it to a stop, just short of the bridge across the Grindstone River.

"For God's sake, save us," screamed an old woman, who, with her two daughters, were the first to reach the train.

"The depot's burning," said another, as he climbed aboard.

"Everything's burning," said others as they rushed into the cars.

"Hurry folks," shouted Root, as he opened the throttle and the reversing valves. "We'll run you back to Skunk Lake."

"It's six miles," McGowan said, shoveling into the firebox. "I hope we make it."

Root could see the bridge starting to burn as he backed away. Then he heard a loud explosion, felt a strong wind in his face, and looked down to see ties start to burn. He looked back and the whole train was showing fingers of fire along the sides of the cars.

Just as Root settled into his seat, still opening the throttle, the heavy glass in the cab window buckled in and broke into a hundred pieces. Later Root would realize that he had been cut severely, but at the time he didn't notice it.

As he approached a cut on top of the Big Hinckley Hill, Root saw three more men running to catch the train. He applied his brakes, thinking to take them on. Then he realized that if he stopped in the cut, the flames would burn his air hose, leaving them stranded there. Reluctantly he opened the throttle again. Still, two of the men caught the front of the engine as it passed, but one of them fell off to burn to death, fairly near to the one who didn't make it.

Then Root passed out from the heat. When he came to, he was alone in the cab. The engine was going very slow, but she still had ninety pounds of steam. Wondering what had become of his fireman, Root pulled himself up to the throttle, opened it, and slid back into the seat.

Just then McGowan showed up. He was completely immersed in the water tank! Root got dizzy again, and McGowan threw water over him.

"That felt good," Root said. "My hands are cooked."

"So are mine," McGowan croaked.

As McGowan began shoveling in more coal, Root noticed some water in the ditch beside the track, and he knew they had reached Skunk Lake. He applied the air and stopped the train. McGowan wanted to help him, but Root told him to help the passengers off the train and into the lake.

By now all the cars were ablaze, both inside and out. Root learned later that every window had been shattered by the heat. Just before reaching the lake, a dozen or more of the three hundred passengers had panicked and leaped off the train. Root thought more of them would have followed except that their porter, John Blair, went through the coaches with a fire extinguisher, squirting it on those whose clothing had caught fire.

After Jack McGowan had the passengers off the train and in the water, he returned to Root and helped him out. By then a total of four hundred and thirty men, women, and children, some of whom had not arrived on the train, were in the water.

"There we sat," Root recalled later. "A few horses and cows had followed us into the lake, and a few deer, a couple of timber wolves, a black bear, and other wild and domestic animals, all cowering and suffering in the water with us. Showers of sparks rained down on our unprotected heads. Flaming boughs and twigs whirled through the dense, over-hot air."

While they watched the coaches burn and waited for the fire to die down a little, Root and McGowan decided to save the engine if they could. They crawled back to the engine, McGowan pulled the coupling pin, and Root ran her ahead a few yards. Everything burnable was already destroyed, but they hoped this would save the rest. Then they hurried back into the water, where they sat with the others for four agonizing hours. They were rescued by volunteers who came through on hand cars.

The Eastern Minnesota had a gravel pit next to its Hinckley depot. About seventy people who were unable to get out of town got into a pool of water in the pit, along with domestic and wild animals, and survived. However a hundred and twenty others, panicky and bewildered, sought shelter in a dry slough which had formerly contained water. They could have gone to the gravel pit or even into the narrow Grindstone River, but they all died, huddled together into a pathetic mass of bodies.

There were many heroes that day. Tom Dunn, telegraph operator for the St. Paul and Duluth, refused to leave his station, so he could handle necessary messages. He perished when the depot burned up. Bull Henley, a section hand, stood in the road while flames burned his clothing and licked his face, helping the confused residents get to the gravel pit. He survived.

Fireman Jack McGowan eventually became an engineer on the Northern Pacific. He was instantly killed when his engine overturned on a softened roadway. At the time of that accident, McGowan was wearing the gold watch that had been presented to him for heroism in the Hinckley fire.

The fires burned for five days after Hinckley's destruction. A rain on September 6 finally stopped them. For months afterward, woodsmen and trappers would find charred bodies in the woods. Four hundred and seventy-six bodies were recovered, including the remains of twenty-two forest-dwelling Indians, before snow put an end to the search.

Twenty-five hundred acres of woods had burned, and the estimated death toll was five hundred.

Suggested reading: Freeman H. Hubbard, *Railroad Avenue* (New York: McGraw Hill, 1945).

THE BROWNIES

Arthur Sitwell first heard the "Brownies" when he was fifteen. He recorded it in his diary: "This unseen voice told me that I would meet and marry a girl named Genevieve Wood. I knew no one by that name, but four years later I met her and we married."

From then on, Arthur never questioned the advice he got from his Brownies. After his marriage, Arthur worked as a clerk in Indiana, but the small voices kept telling him to go west and build a railroad. He reached Kansas City with his new bride and the clothes on his back.

Kansas City was booming. Arthur found work clerking in a brokerage house. After branching out into real estate and insurance, he purchased an interest in an amusement park in the late 1880s. But the park was not easy to reach from Kansas City.

The Brownies started their chant, "Build a railroad, build a railroad." Arthur got backing and soon had a profitable railroad and an interest in a profitable amusement park.

But as he settled back to enjoy his wealth, the Brownies continued their agitation, "Build a railroad, build a railroad."

But where? The answer came as he was reading one night: Connect the Kansas wheat fields with the Gulf of Mexico.

Arthur got backing and began the Kansas City, Pittsburg and Gulf line, later called the Kansas City Southern. The rails crossed the Kansas plains, the eastern part of Indian Territory, and eastern Texas toward the destination of Galveston.

But as the construction moved south from Houston in late 1899, Arthur Sitwell suddenly ordered work to stop. His astonished crew, so near their destination, wondered if the boss had been hearing the Brownies again.

He had. They had told him to stop at Sabine Lake, make that his terminal, and name it after himself. Arthur didn't think much of the advice or of the lake as a terminal, but he had learned to obey, so Port Arthur became the terminal of the railroad.

Less than a year later, on September 8, 1900, a hurricane destroyed half of Galveston and took six thousand lives. Port Arthur was untouched, and the railroad helped greatly in rescue work.

But Arthur got into a fight with one of his backers, John "Bet a Million" Gates, and when it ended Gates owned the railroad and most of the land around Port Arthur.

Arthur's depression was short-lived. As he got up to give a speech in Kansas City that he was through with railroads, he seemed to go into a trance. The crowd was startled to hear him call for a map of the United States and a long piece of string.

Arthur suddenly announced, "I will build a railroad that will bring the Pacific closer to Kansas City by four hundred miles. His Brownies had spoken again, and Arthur started construction of the Kansas City, Mexico, and Orient at Emporia, Kansas, on July 4, 1901.

To reach his destination at the port of Topolobampo, Arthur would have to use the Mexican Central Railroad, which was owned by the Mexican government. He thought the project was worth the risk of dealing with a volatile government.

"It's a natural port for large ships," Arthur said. "They have seventeen feet of water over the harbor bar at low tide. Besides mining treasures from the Rockies and Mexico, we'll haul fruit and vegetables from Texas. Their season is a month earlier than California, and the Orient trade is ours for the taking."

Arthur talked with Porfirio Diaz about the project, and the Mexican dictator agreed with the plan and offered a subsidy of five thousand dolars a mile for construction.

But Arthur had trouble from the beginning. Pancho Villa had a contract for grading, and he and Arthur hated each other. Arthur called him a "dirty, greasy fellow."

When the revolution began, Villa took great delight in blowing up Arthur's tracks. When the line went into receivership, the Santa Fe bought the trackage in the United States. Once again, Arthur had lost a railroad.

Finally, the Brownies stopped insisting that Arthur build more railroads. But if you asked an engineer today to draw the shortest route from Kansas City to the Pacific, he would draw the same one the Brownies drew.

"They showed me the way," Arthur maintained, "but I was only a mortal man and I fell short of their goals."

Suggested reading: Mary Ann Smith, "Brownies that Founded a Railroad," in *The West* (March, 1970).

ORDERING INFORMATION

True Tales of the Old West
is projected for 40 volumes.

For Titles in Print —
Ask at your bookstore
or write:

PIONEER PRESS
P. O. Box 216
Carson City, NV 89702-0216
(775) 888-9867
FAX (775) 888-0908

Other titles in progress include:

Pioneer Children	Frontier Courts & Lawyers
Old West Riverboaters	Frontier Artists
Army Women	Californios
Western Duelists	Early West Explorers
Government Leaders	Homesteaders
Early Lumbermen	Old West Merchants
Frontier Militiamen	Scientists & Engineers
Preachers & Spirit Guides	Frontier Teachers
Teamsters & Packers	Visitors to the Frontier
Doctors & Healers	Storms & Floods
Mysteries & Ghosts	Wild Animals